THE LITTLE BOOK OF
CRAFT BEER

MELISSA COLE

A GUIDE TO OVER 100 OF
THE WORLD'S FINEST BREWS

Illustrated by Stuart Hardie

hardie grant books

DEDICATION

To Glenn Payne: I wouldn't be where I am today without your friendship and patronage; I miss you terribly.

To Joshua Arnold: as I finish this book it's your 18th birthday. You're a remarkable young man already; I can't wait to see what you do with your life and I hope you'll always have time for a pint with your Auntie Minibus.

CONTENTS

FOREWORD   7

INTRODUCTION   8

RAW INGREDIENTS   10

BEER AND FOOD   18

CHAPTER ONE: LAGERS   20

CHAPTER TWO: SESSION BEERS   34

CHAPTER THREE: WHEATS, WITS AND WEIZENS   44

CHAPTER FOUR: HOP STARS   58

CHAPTER FIVE: RED, AMBER AND BROWN   72

CHAPTER SIX: SPICE UP YOUR LIFE   88

CHAPTER SEVEN: FRUIT BEERS   100

CHAPTER EIGHT: FARMHOUSE BEERS   112

CHAPTER NINE: WILD AND TAMED ONES   122

CHAPTER TEN: THE DARK SIDE   134

CHAPTER ELEVEN: BIG BEERS   148

CHAPTER TWELVE: NO, LOW AND G-FREE BEERS   158

AUTHOR BIOGRAPHY   170

ACKNOWLEDGEMENTS   171

INDEX   172

FOREWORD

By John Keeling, Director of Brewing, Fuller's Brewery

The world of beer now values flavour above all considerations and this is why you have chosen the right book, as Melissa is an expert in flavour – which is also why I have invited her twice to brew beers with me.

Now, you might wonder 'why does a brewer need to collaborate with a writer to make a beer?' Firstly, it's because Melissa is a person of many opinions and I value those opinions, both as a friend and in my role as brewing director of Fuller, Smith & Turner; I don't always agree with her but that is quite natural because nobody has exactly the same taste.

But mostly it's because of her innate understanding of flavour and which ones work together, and how, that makes her insights invaluable, especially in modern brewing, where so many non-traditional ingredients are used. It is very useful indeed to have someone like Melissa around because between her palate, experience of cooking and judging beer competitions the world over, her knowledge is as broad as it is deep.

In these pages I'm proud that you'll find mention of both Fuller's Imperial Stout and Vintage Ale (see pages 141 and 153). The inspiration for Vintage originally came from the Fuller's marketing team, which proves that inspiration can come from unusual places! However, as all good stories should start, one day in the pub Melissa raised the idea of wanting to brew a Turkish delight beer, and it was just so crazy that we had to brew it (it does help that we'd had a few beers to lubricate the thought process too!).

But collaborations are just a small part of the value Melissa gives to brewers and beer enthusiasts; I always find the discussions about beer that we have over a pint are not only enlightening, but also inspire me to make better beer.

So, I hope you find this book enlightening too and, most importantly, I hope it inspires you to explore beer more, by trying some of the food recipes and beer matches because you have chosen an excellent guide.

INTRODUCTION

I want to be very upfront with you here, because... well, the intro seems the logical place to do this. This is not a book for beer nerds.

Don't get me wrong: I would love for established beer lovers to have this book on their shelf, but it's not designed to teach them much more than they already know. This is a book for people who want to begin their journey in beer. It's a starter to make everyone who picks it up thirsty, inquisitive and slightly better informed, but not so overwhelmed with technical jargon that it sends them running in the opposite direction!

Sure, there is a bit of techy, geeky stuff, but what are books like this for other than to provide you with some info to show off to friends and win pub quizzes with?

There are also lots of breweries that I'd love to have in here and whose omission is bound to cause grumbling, many of

them darlings of the cognoscenti. But the way innovation in the beer world has gone means that some fabulous breweries rarely, if ever, repeat their beers.

This makes it impossible to write an accessible book, send it for editing, then to print, and then six months later have anyone find the beer I'm talking about! It's not that I don't love what these yeast-wrangling maniacs are doing, I do, it's just they live in a different and rarefied atmosphere from the one I'm sharing here.

All I hoped to do was create a great gateway guide, something that includes beers that you may have to seek out and ones that you will increasingly see on the shelves of your local stores as they catch on to the global zeitgeist that is 'craft beer'*.

Beyond the drinking side, I'm also a passionate advocate of beer and food pairing and cooking with beer, which

I've been doing seriously for about eight years now. My philosophy about cooking with beer is that I don't use a beer just because; it has to lend something to the dish. It has to earn its keep.

I don't subscribe to just using beer because your recipe needs a liquid. I would rather drink it and appreciate it than dump it in a pot for no good reason, which is why each section has its own specific, simple recipe.

I've also, just for fun, included a cocktail for most sections, which can be a great way of getting friends into beer who might not necessarily try it, or to use a second bottle of beer that you didn't really care for by itself, or just because you've had a crappy day at the office and feel like dancing around in your pyjamas with something a bit fancy.

All of these are perfectly valid reasons to gussy up your brew. So whether, as a result of reading this book, you just

try a different lager, hoover more hops than you ever have done before, single out the sours or just embrace your dark side, I'll be thrilled.

Oh, and be sure to come and find me on social media to let me know how your journey is going (see page 19).

*No, I'm not sure what really is or isn't craft beer. All I'm going to say is that after 12 years of writing about beer, 10 years of judging it internationally and 9 years of occasional brewing, I'd like to think I know a quality brew when I taste it, regardless of ownership, and I would never, ever mislead others into trying something I didn't personally rate. I take beer very seriously, so you don't have to (plus I have that being raised a Catholic 'guilt' thing too!)

RAW INGREDIENTS

The soul of any beer is its raw ingredients and every single one has a vital part to play.

In today's hop-obsessed beer market, you could be forgiven for thinking that nothing else matters, but just as it's often the unsung ingredient, like perfect seasoning, that makes all the difference to a fantastic plate of food, so it is with beers.

Brews that are carefully constructed for all the ingredients to work in harmony are often the best; it's a bit like a great band: just because one member will occasionally step forward for a solo doesn't mean the rest of the band isn't still there backing them up!

GRAINS

The structure on which every beer stands is its malt base, but what is malt exactly? To put it really simply, it's a grain, normally barley, that's been fooled into thinking it's springtime to start germination, and then stopped in its tracks by a careful drying and toasting process.

The level to which you toast the grains in the malting process gives you not only lots of accessible starches and active enzymes in the grains – the latter of which will convert the starches into sugars for the yeast to munch on and produce alcohol – but also accounts for colour and flavour in your beer.

The flavours (and colours) from malts can range from the lightest white bread, through wholemeal, to caramel and toffee, to raisin and milk chocolate to dark chocolate, through to the deepest espresso. These can then be mixed with a host of other malted and unmalted grains like wheat, oats, sorghum, rye and others

to create as simple or as complex a flavour profile as you could wish for.

The very best malting barley is considered to come from maritime climates, and the UK is said by most brewers to have the best in the world (although, of course, that may also be a little bit of the good kind of national pride talking!).

FACT: Maris Otter is a species of barley grown in the UK that is famous the world over. The first species of barley that was deliberately bred for making beer, it is still prized for its flavour more than 50 years after being introduced.

WATER

Water, water everywhere – but not for making beer... well, OK, that's not strictly true, but if you want to lay a bit of beer knowledge on people, then you can tell them that in the brew house, the water used for brewing is called 'liquor' and 'water' is used for washing things. I know, it's all a bit unnecessarily complicated, but that's brewers for you!

One of the reasons for differentiating is that brewers regularly treat the water they get, often from the mains, with what are known as 'brewer's salts'.

This is the process of treating the water with different minerals to mimic the natural water source of classic beer styles.

So, for example, one of the reasons that Burton-on-Trent became renowned for its IPAs is that its natural water source is very rich in gypsum, or calcium sulphate as it's scientifically known, which creates a more pronounced dry, clean bitterness.

Whereas London, historically renowned for its porters, is known to have a calcium carbonate-rich water supply, more suited to malt-forward beers and creating a rounder mouthfeel. Alternatively, you could class them as soft and hard waters respectively, but where's the fun nerd factor in that?

HOPS

'A wicked and pernicious weed,' said someone at some point, although contrary to myth and legend, there is no evidence it was King Henry VI... but it's still an accurate description of the hop.

It is a climbing plant, which, if you look closely, can often be found running wild in hedgerows and even urban settings (near me in south-west London there's an alleyway with a rather large and luxuriant hop plant that's been left to grow untamed). However, its use in, and cultivation for, modern brewing now means that hops are used in nearly all but the tiniest percentage of the world's beer.

Hops, like grapes, develop a terroir. In case you were frightened to ask anyone what terroir means (like me when I first heard it) it's the effect that the hours of sunlight, the soil and the general climate has on a crop. In this case I'm talking about hops, but you'll more generally hear it spoken of in terms of wines.

Regardless of their original species, within a decade or so of having been planted in a different country, hops will develop characteristics that are so far away from their forebears that they are often renamed. For example, NZ Cascade has now been renamed Taiheke, but it originated from the Cascade hop that first came from a cross between a UK hop and a European hop. Every step of the way has been important in the development of that hop's characteristics, but the defining factor in what it smells and tastes like today is the terroir that it has been shaped by most recently.

Anyway, my point is that hops have followed a similar path to that of 'old' and 'new world' wines a few decades ago, which brings us neatly back to that word 'terroir'.

Traditionally the UK has been known for its subtly bitter hops, with restrained aroma characteristics like tobacco, hedgerow

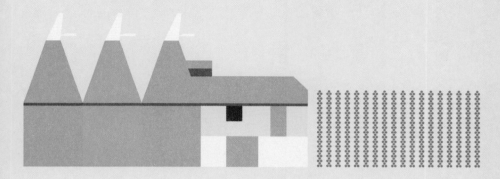

fruit and mown grass. A lot of Central and Eastern European hops have similar characteristics to UK hops, but many of them have also been developed specifically for delicate styles like Pilsners and other lagers or ales, so you get more subtle and restrained notes like woody herbs, black pepper and fresh hay.

The USA is known for its more aggressively bitter hops, with big citrus, pine, rose and marijuana aromas and flavours. Australian hops tend towards the US versions with some fairly hefty bitterness, but with more subtle apricot, peach, lemony flavours and aromas and the odd foray into more floral lands.

Then there are New Zealand hops, which have some of the most interesting and complex flavours being developed anywhere (in my opinion). Their bitterness can be subtle to booming and aromas and flavours range from Sauvignon Blanc to lime zest, cherry blossom and beyond.

DID YOU KNOW... Just as growers in 'old world' wine countries like France and Spain have started to develop lighter, more accessible and often more tropical flavours, so have 'old world' hop-growing countries like the UK, Germany the Czech Republic turned to 'new world' countries like the USA, Australia, New Zealand and Canada to ape their very popular hop characteristics.

YEASTS AND BEASTS

Yeast, that beautiful single-celled fungus that takes in sugars and expels alcohol and carbon dioxide, is the most critical ingredient in beer that was considered a magical element before science identified its presence.

Ancient civilisations believed that deities gifted the alcoholic element of their brews, the most famous evidence for which is the Hymn to Ninkasi, the Sumerian goddess of beer. The praise for this goddess was immortalised in a stone tablet in 1800 BC and also doubles up as a recipe for beer. And even the infamous Rheinheitsgebot, the German Purity Law, didn't recognise yeast as one of the core ingredients of beer when the first draft was written in Bavaria in the early 1500s. But now, thanks to technology, we understand more about yeast than we ever have before.

Yeasts are now so diverse that it's difficult to explain things simply, but here are the main types of the Saccharomyces family.

LAGER YEASTS

The strain of yeast most commonly used for lagers is Saccharomyces pastorianus (named for Louis Pasteur who identified it as the most efficient yeast to make cold maturation beers). These diligent yeasts like to operate at cool temperatures over a week or so and then, quite literally, chill out for a few weeks, by which I mean stay in cold storage (this is where we actually get the word 'lager' from – it's derived from the German word to store).

ALE YEASTS

Saccharomyces cerevisiae usually likes warmer temperatures and will ferment quickly, without the need to be held at very cold temperatures for a long time. These yeasts tend to create fruity or spicy flavours and don't eat all the complex sugars, so leave a little more of a rounded mouthfeel.

BEASTS

There are also some other microscopic organisms that like to get in on the act. Brettanomyces is one of them. Meaning 'British fungus', it was first classified from British porters and is what is responsible for the 'funk' in certain beer. Much slower to act than other yeasts, it also tends to eat up all the sugars that its faster-acting cousin leaves behind, resulting in a bracing dryness and complex aromas ranging from high tropical notes to sweaty horse blankets (the latter not always terribly desirable!) You will find it in Lambic-style beers and some saisons and imperial stouts (although it's used more widely today by experimental brewers, this is where you will find it traditionally).

Finally, the bit that may freak you out a little, but please bear with me here! There can also be bacteria involved in making beers... WAIT, don't run away. The main strain that is used is also the stuff that makes yoghurt, which is called Lactobacillus and provides a lovely zingy sourness, the key characteristics of beer styles like Berliner Weisse or Gose. And there's also something called Pediococcus, which produces a stronger sourness. Finally, very occasionally, you'll find Acetobacter as well, but that is extremely rare and found only in very few beer styles due to its aggressive nature – after all, not a lot of people appreciate vinegary beer!

BEER AND FOOD

Beer and food are the most natural of partners. From simple pairings like a ploughman's and a pint to more esoteric offerings like ale roast duck and barley wine, you can run the full gamut of tasty tie-ups.

But how do you start? Well, the first thing to remember is the old Army acronym K.I.S.S. – keep it simple, stupid.

Not that I'm calling you lovely people stupid, it's just that this is the most intelligent way to approach things, by starting simply and building confidence and knowledge of your palate and its preferred pairings from there.

The first bit of 'homework' for you is to get to know your beer. How intense is it in flavour? If it's a subtle, good-quality lager or a soft golden ale, then you want to keep your food very simple. Consider using just a few herbs and a bit of citrus, like a simple piece of white fish with a touch of

thyme and a few slices of lemon, perhaps baked in a paper parcel with a splash of your chosen beer to steam it in, or maybe a goat's cheese salad.

If you are ramping up the flavours a bit with a Belgian-style wheat beer, which traditionally uses coriander seeds and orange peel in the recipe, then sushi or moules à la bière (moules marinière but replacing the wine with Belgian wheat beer) is a great way to go. As you get a bit more complex with the malt profile of your beer, such as subtle UK-style bitters or brown ales, you can introduce a more toasted character to your food.

A great Welsh rarebit/rabbit (a historic debate I'm not going into here!) or a fabulous rare roast beef sandwich with just a lick of horseradish and some peppery watercress could be your friend. Wandering more into the highly hopped territory of pale ales and IPAs, you need to go sweeter, so the classic pulled pork with tonnes of

caramelised onions is a real winner (just make sure it's not too spicy unless you are a chilli masochist, as the hops and CO_2 in your beer will exacerbate the heat more and more as you eat and drink).

Sometimes, when the beer is really tropical in its hopping, using varieties like Mosaic or Citra, you can opt for vanilla ice cream with mango and passion fruit coulis drizzled over the top for a full fandango of fruity flavour. Then, as we get to the darker side, you must consider how much roasted bitterness your beer has. Deep-roasted stouts need to be balanced with sweetness, like milk chocolate; whereas bigger, boozier, sweeter offerings like barley wines and old ales can be used to balance out very salty foodstuffs, like big blue cheeses or a salt cod stew.

As more sour beer styles become available, you can use their acidity to balance out rich, indulgent flavours. Try slow-cooked beef cheeks with a dark sour beer that also has some earthiness from Brettanomyces yeast, like a Flanders-style red, or perhaps use a lighter, fruited Berliner Weisse as a match for a Christmas feast of partridge and pickled pears. And, of course, fruited sour beers are wonderful with indulgent chocolate desserts, helping to cut through their rich, cloying nature. However, that does also allow you to eat more pudding – a good or bad thing depending on your view of your waistline!

Throughout the book there are recipes using different beer styles and some suggested matches to go with them, so whether you opt to use those or head in your own direction, I'd love for you to let me know how you get on. Please do send me pictures and messages via social media of your beer and food fun (because that's what it should be, heaps of fun).

Twitter: @melissacole
Facebook & Instagram: @melissacolebeer
Web: www.melissacolebeer.com

CHAPTER ONE

LAGER

What defines a beer as a lager? Well, 'lagering' is actually the term for an extended period of ageing the beer at a very cold temperature.

However, we have come to see lager through the lens of styles like Pilsner, which is the inspiration for most of the world's best-selling beers (albeit most of them are no longer properly lagered).

Lager comes in all shapes and forms, from Oktoberfests (for which you should travel to Munich and the festival to try them at their best) to Dunkels, black lagers to commodity brands and far beyond.

I've tried to incorporate a few different styles in here, and you'll also find a Bock beer in the Red, Amber and Brown chapter.

So, I'd like to encourage you to spread your wings beyond the norm with this style of beer and to try beers that have a bit more (in some cases a lot more) flavour than the well-known, rather watered-down brands.

CROUCHER NEW ZEALAND PILSNER

ABV
5%

Country of origin
New Zealand

Try it if you like
Light, dry tropical wines

Great with
Simple grilled shellfish

Also try
Five Points Pils
4.8%, UK

What started off as a typical Czech-inspired Pils has, with the addition of those super-fruity New Zealand hops, morphed into something more akin to the love child of a Pilsner and a pale ale.

And it's a real achievement from this tiny brewery in an industrial estate in Rotorua, which has some of the most innovative solutions to brewing on a shoestring I've ever seen. However, the welcome was anything other than parsimonious, especially in its tap house in the town where they serve great beer and food.

Zesty and tropical but still providing all the refreshing qualities you want from a lager, it is one that I genuinely hanker after on hot days.

Unfortunately the brewery is halfway around the world from me, but I would happily travel for it, as it's one of the most quaffable beers I've had in my entire life.

LA CUMBRE BEER

ABV
4.7%

Country of origin
USA

Try it if you like
Prosecco

Great with
A hot sunny day

Also try
7Peaks La Dent Jaune
5.2%, Switzerland

Like everyone else, I have little rituals, silly daft things that make me happy, and one of those things involves this beer. It's always, always the first beer I drink when I get into the Great American Beer Festival, and brewmaster Jeff Erway knows to start pouring the minute he sees me coming!

You might be wondering why: why is this beer so special? After all, it's 'just a lager', right?

Wrong. There's a reason why brewers and beer writers like me love a great lager. First and foremost it's because to brew a truly great lager, without any flaws, is one of the hardest skills in brewing.

It's also because when you've been judging everything from imperial barrel-aged stouts to smoke beers for three days, there is nothing, and I mean nothing, finer than a brilliantly crafted lager like this.

Clean, fresh and full of flavour, it demands nothing more of you than to enjoy its zesty, zippy, lemony refreshment and incredibly clean fermentation and maturation – just like it should be.

LOST AND GROUNDED RUNNING WITH SCEPTRES

ABV
5.2%

Country of origin
UK

Try it if you like
Champagne

Great with
A fresh pretzel

Also try
Forst Felsenkeller
5.2%, Italy

When Alex Troncoso, formerly of Little Creatures in Australia and Camden Town Brewery in London, announced he was opening a brewery in Bristol with his partner Annie Clements, the beer world was waiting with pint glasses at dawn for the first brews, and they didn't disappoint.

The Keller Pils (cellar Pils) is a triumph because there are so few beers made in this style that package well, but Lost and Grounded have achieved it without filtering or fining, thus leaving a lot of the delicious bready character that comes with the German Pilsner style.

Being true to the style, they have also used typical German hops, meaning that there's a lot of cut-grass character and that lovely scrubby, herbaceous thing they have going on.

PILSNER URQUELL

ABV
4.4%

Country of origin
Czech Republic

Try it if you like
Peroni

Great with
Another one!

Also try
Birrificio Italiano Tipopils
5.2%, Italy

You simply can't write a section on lager and leave out Pilsner Urquell, the brewery that spawned a thousand imitators and gave birth to the world's favourite beer style (albeit most of them are now pale imitations of where it all started).

The story of how this beer was created is no doubt somewhat sanitised and far from the reality, but the rough gist of it all is that the town of Pilsen was so disgusted with the beer that was being made there that in 1838 they poured it down the drain, drummed the brewer out of town and hired an angry young man called Josef Groll who had knowledge of English pale malting techniques and German lager yeast to come and brew at the brewery that was being built. In October 1842 the first beer was poured and everyone was delighted. It gained a reputation and the rest, as they say, is history.

Although I mentioned pale malt you'll note that PU (as it's affectionately called) is actually a golden hue. That's because they boil part of the wort in separate vessels to get the distinctive caramelisation in the beer. Add to that the local Saaz hops and a five-week lagering time and you have simple drinking perfection.

KÖSTRITZER SCHWARZBIER

ABV
4.8%

Country of origin
Germany

Try it if you like
Porters

Great with
Slow-cooked pork knuckle

Also try
Thornbridge Lukas
4.2%, UK

Köstritzer is one of the oldest producers of Schwarzbier (black lager) in the world and it does it extremely well.

A true survivor of the Berlin Wall, it was one of the few German breweries that managed to keep up exports from East Germany during the great divide with the West.

Now owned by German brewing giant Bitburger, it still continues to turn out the most moreish of all the black lagers in my opinion, with dried fruit and coffee notes and a hint of fresh tobacco. It is definitely one to try if you think that dark beer can't be light and refreshing.

FIRESTONE WALKER PIVO HOPPY PILS

ABV
5.3%

Country of origin
USA

Try it if you like
Real lemonade

Great with
Lobster

Also try
Himburg's Braukunst
Keller Bavarian
Dry Hop Lager
5.3%, Germany

Firestone Walker produces so many great beers, it's genuinely hard to narrow it down to just this one, but if you really twisted my arm, this would always be the one I'd go for.

Created by brewmaster Matt Brynildson, widely regarded in the industry as one of the most talented and knowledgeable guys around, the beer takes influences from both the European and US brewing industries to create an aromatic and refreshing delight of a brew.

This beer is influenced by the British-influenced American love of dry-hopping beers to get big aroma from the hops. Here German Saphir hops provide hints of Amalfi lemon and lemongrass, making it as enticing on the nose as it is smooth on the palate.

AUGUSTINER-BRÄU DUNKEL

ABV
5.6%

Country of origin
Germany

Try it if you like
British bitters

Great with
Schnitzel

Also try
Calvors Dark Dunkel Lager
4.5%, UK

Dunkel is the classic, historic style of Munich and Augustiner is one of its finest proponents. One of the six official breweries that can produce Oktoberfest beers for the famous Munich piss up – sorry, celebration – Augustiner knows what it is doing when it comes to making lagers, given that they've been brewing since 1328.

Run by monks for 500 years, the monastery went into state ownership in 1803 due to the secular reform happening in the country and then it moved into private hands, and moved out of the crumbling monastery, in 1817 and, despite having a few different sites in that time, remains Munich through and through.

Light coffee and chocolate notes are augmented by a fresh cut grass and herbal hop character but all in a really light, easy-drinking body, so don't be afraid of the colour, just enjoy the different experience of drinking a dark lager.

BEERY TEMPURA

Serves 4–6 as an appetiser

1.25 kg (2 lb 7 oz) fish or
    750 g (1 lb 10 oz) seafood or
    vegetables of choice, such as
    carrots, cut into 2 cm (20 mm)
    batons
sea salt
groundnut (peanut) or
    grapeseed oil, for frying

For the tempura batter
ice cubes
200 g (7 oz/1⅓ cups) plain
    (all-purpose) flour
200 g (7 oz/1⅔ cups) cornflour
    (cornstarch)
1 medium egg
200 ml (7 fl oz/¾ cup)
    good-quality lager,
    put in the freezer until
    just about to freeze

I've not specified what you use the batter for here, because you can make your tempura with finely cut vegetables, thin strips of fish, whole prawns (shrimp) or scallops. Whatever you choose, make sure that you have two metal bowls that fit inside each other and plenty of ice to hand.

Prep the fish, seafood or vegetables and season lightly with sea salt. Place a wire mesh rack over a baking tray in a just warm oven and heat the oil in a deep fryer (this is safest) or a wok to 170°C (340°F).

To make the batter, first start by placing a layer of ice in the first, larger metal bowl (see intro above) and cover with a layer of paper towel.

Put the flours in the second, smaller metal bowl and mix well. Place the flour bowl inside the ice bowl.

Mix in the egg and beer lightly with chopsticks. Don't overmix – there should be lumps.

Dip your seasoned fish, seafood or vegetables in the batter and fry, without overloading the fryer, until light gold and crispy. Season lightly just before serving.

BEERITA SUNRISE

3 parts cold fresh lemonade
3 parts cold lager
3 parts tequila blanco
1 part grenadine
cocktail umbrella, to garnish
(because it's silly and fun!)

As this is a great party cocktail I've given the recipe in parts – so you can make as much or as little as you wish.

Pour the lemonade, lager and tequila into a jug or large glass and stir gently. Pour into tall glasses.

Very gently pour the grenadine down the inside of each glass. One of those fancy, swirly bartender's spoons is good for this. It will swirl slightly with the bubbles but will mostly sink to the bottom, giving that sunrise effect.

Serve with the umbrella and drink while imagining you're on a beach in Mexico.

CHAPTER TWO

SESSION BEERS

What defines a session beer exactly? Well, this is a matter of much debate around the world, but despite how well travelled I am, I am still a Brit who likes to drink pints and for me it means around 4.5% or below. However, I have snuck in a few exceptions because, try as I might, I can't get the whole of the brewing industry to agree with me!

I'm seeing a huge move in the 'craft beer' sector back to lower ABV beers, whether that's with subtle, delicate Berliner Weisses or brightly aromatic but delicately bitter beers, like I've focused on here.

And that's a good thing all round for artisan beer's wider appeal. After all, there are only so many Imperial Stouts or DIPAs that a girl (or guy) can drink before losing their taste buds! But the overarching reason I'm pleased about this move is because my personal philosophy about beer is that it should serve primarily as a social lubricant.

When all is said and done, the beers I enjoy most are the three or four (or more when I'm being naughty) that I have with friends in a pub, at a beer festival or wherever, and I really like to drink those and not fall over. It might not be the classiest of definitions, but you know what I mean, right? God, I hope my mum isn't reading this!

FOURPURE SESSION IPA

ABV
4.2%

Country of origin
UK

Try it if you like
Albariño

Great with
Lamb burger,
strawberry cheesecake

Also try
Founders All Day IPA
4.7%, USA

This little beer has a huge place in my heart for its sheer drinkability – and the fact that it's a home town brew for me too.

The Fourpure crew lives and breathes the brewery's beers and you'd be hard pushed to meet a more enthusiastic and friendly bunch of people, in fact you can generally tell where they are from the cries of 'Fourpure Fam For Life' - I'm sure they spell it in a much cooler way than that, but that's because they are all about 20 years younger than me!

Anyway, back to the beer! Perfect in can or on keg, it ticks every box that you want it to when thinking about a session beer; light of body, full of gentle strawberry, papaya and lime zest, and with the shortest, most refreshing of finishes, it disappears like a lover in the night who leaves you wanting more.

LAGUNITAS DAYTIME ALE

ABV
4.7%

Country of origin
USA

Try it if you like
Blonde ales

Great with
Pork burger

Also try
Edge Brewing Ziggy
4.8%, Spain

Lagunitas is a brewery with a brilliant maverick at the helm in the shape of Tony Magee, a man who when other people go left, he goes off on an angle.

Which is why DayTime is, rather typically, not called session IPA or a session beer but a Fractional IPA because, why would Tony do anything that everyone else is doing? It could possibly be partially through the assistance of hop's closest relative that all these things come to him but who can tell?

DayTime is quite different from a lot of other session IPAs in that it has a lot more body than most, with rich rye bread and brioche flavours, overlaid with a delicate rose, candied grapefruit peel and lime aroma and flavour.

And, as advertised, if you paced yourself you probably could, indeed, drink it all day – although the suggestion on the website that it can be had with breakfast is probably not to be recommended!

DOUGALL'S 942

ABV
4.2%

Country of origin
Spain

Try it if you like
Verdejo

Great with
Padron peppers

Also try
Hornbeer Top Hop
4.7%, Denmark

Brewery co-owner Andrew Dougall is a British expat who is properly living the dream. Opening up his brewery not far from Santander, he's as happy as a clam, or should I say happy as an almeja?

I firmly believe that he was dreaming of lying on the beach, as opposed to working in a hot brewery, when he came up with this beer, because I can't imagine a better place to be drinking it.

A really simple two-malt, two-hop recipe, it is like a mix between a pale ale and a lager, making it perfect for its home environment or for when you're just dreaming of sun, sea, sand and session IPA (which, in my case, is about seven times a day).

GARAGE PROJECT HĀPI DAZE

ABV
4.6%

Country of origin
New Zealand

Try it if you like
New Zealand Sauvignon Blanc

Great with
Freshly caught trout

Also try
Dugges All the Way
4.2%, Sweden

Hāpi is the Maori word for hop, which cheers me up immensely because hops used like this make me deliriously... well... happy!

The terroir of New Zealand hops is something I've had the privilege to experience first hand, and a lot of the stops that I made on my three weeks across the country's two incredibly beautiful islands involved sipping one of these at some point, because of its immense drinkability.

Full of the aromas and flavours of lemongrass, Sauvignon Blanc, bergamot, orange and coriander seed, it is a beer I could happily drink all day long.

Unfortunately it didn't help me catch a trout, which is why I dream of drinking one while cooking a fish I've landed by burying it in the hot sands of Lake Tarawera – sigh.

THE WHITE HAG LITTLE FAWN SESSION IPA

ABV
4.2%

Country of Origin
Ireland

Try it if you like
Rubicon

Great with
New York cheesecake

Also try
Cerveceria Agua Mala
Session IPA
4%, Mexico

I love the fact that in Irish mythology the hag is an elemental goddess connected with the harvest, seasons and the weather, which are all so intrinsically linked with brewing.

Part of a very quickly expanding Irish craft brewing scene, this brewery is one to watch in my opinion, turning out one of the best quality ranges of beers from the Emerald Isle.

The first thing you notice is the huge passion fruit nose on this beer, which reminded me instantly of the fizzy passion fruit drink Rubicon. When you dive in you get a soft, rounded body that's elevated by the slightly restrained carbonation and then finishes off on a delightfully short and pithy grapefruit note, which makes you just want to dive back in for more.

ASPARAGUS WITH SESSION IPA HOLLANDAISE FOAM

Serves 2 as a starter

8 asparagus spears
2 tablespoons groundnut
(peanut) oil
fine sea salt

For the hollandaise foam
1 teaspoon cider vinegar
2 sprigs of thyme
1 unwaxed lemon, skin peeled
into rough strips and then
juice the fruit
5 black peppercorns
125 g (4 oz/½ cup)
unsalted butter
2 egg yolks
sea salt
1 bottle/can of session
IPA (needs to be ice cold)

Very warm plates play a big role in this dish – make sure you prepare them!

Start by making the hollandaise foam. Put a small saucepan over a medium heat and add the vinegar, thyme, lemon and peppercorns. When it is just bubbling, remove the pan from the heat and set aside to infuse.

Take a small heavy-based saucepan and gently melt the butter over a medium heat, skimming any solids off the top. Remove from the heat and cover to keep warm.

Prepare the asparagus by bending the stems until they snap, then wash thoroughly. Place a chargrill pan over a medium-high heat. Put the asparagus spears in a bowl with some oil and a little salt and toss until well coated. Place the oiled spears on the hot chargrill pan. Once cooked, place on a warmed plate and cover to keep warm.

Strain the infused vinegar and lemon juice mixture into a metal bowl with the egg yolks, sprinkle with a pinch of salt and add a splash of ice-cold beer. Place the bowl on top of a pan of simmering water, making sure that the bowl does not touch the water, and start whisking briskly.

Remove from the heat and gradually add the melted butter until you have a rich, creamy hollandaise. Taste the hollandaise for seasoning and acidity. Add another splash of ice-cold beer and use an electric hand whisk (or a coffee frother) to turn it into a lighter, foamier sauce.

Spoon the sauce over the asparagus and eat with your fingers with a cold glass of the session IPA.

A QUICK SESSION

2 parts vodka,
  straight from the freezer
3 parts well-chilled grapefruit juice
2 parts well-chilled session IPA

Based on the classic Greyhound cocktail, hence the terrible pun, this is a simple and refreshing drink. It's great to make in large quantities for parties, so I've given you the recipe in parts.

Mix the vodka and grapefruit juice, pour into a highball glass and top up carefully with the beer.

You can also put a salt rim on the glass for a take on the Salty Dog.

CHAPTER THREE

WITS, WHEATS AND WEIZENS

Wheat beers can cover such a range of flavours it seems almost rude to plonk them all into the same category, as I could wax lyrical about them all day.

Often you'll hear these beers categorised as Belgian or German in style, with the more recent addition of American-style, too. To be honest, the American-style wheat beer is often fairly unremarkable in that it doesn't have any huge yeast character or additional ingredients, but it is deliciously thirst quenching – Goose Island 312 being a great example.

In contrast, Belgian wheat beers, while generally delicate, traditionally use the addition of coriander seeds and orange peel notes, and German wheat beers have everything from banana to clove to bubble gum in their make-up, depending on the strain of yeast used to make them.

Clear or cloudy, poured with a billowing head or a more subdued foam, however the beer presents, the key criterion is that 30–70 per cent of the grain bill* should be made up of malted or unmalted wheat to give it good body.

* the grain part of the recipe

BRASSERIE LEFEBVRE BLANCHE DE BRUXELLES

ABV
4.5%

Country of origin
Belgium

Try it if you like
Viognier or vodka
and tonic with lemon

Great with
Sashimi

Also try
Brasserie du Bocq
Blanche de Namur
4.5%, France

Stripped of their brewing vessels by the Germans in World War I and nearly put out of business by them again in World War II, the Lefebvre family have demonstrated a commitment to brewing that few could boast.

It seems almost ridiculous to me that Blanche de Bruxelles was only created in 1989 as it's such a world classic, personifying everything that a Belgian wheat beer should be – soft, billowing citrus, light spicy notes and a short refreshing finish.

In case you were wondering, the use of spices in Belgian-style wheat beers is a happy hangover from parts of the Dutch empire.

CAMDEN GENTLEMAN'S WIT

ABV
4.3%

Country of origin
UK

Try it if you like
Earl Grey

Great with
Gin (seriously, the beer makes a very nice 'tonic')

Also try
Feral Brewing Co. White 4.7%, Australia

Camden Town Brewery started as a twinkle in former owner Jasper Cuppaidge's eye in 2010 and built itself quite the reputation, until it was bought by global beer giant ABInbev in 2015 and, as I write, nothing has changed about the beers that I can tell... in fact, I'd go as far as to say that the Pale has significantly improved recently, so let's hope that lasts.

Gentleman's Wit is the result of a very British obsession with tea meeting Belgian brewing tradition. This aromatic brew apes Earl Grey tea's use of bergamot, a fruit I once heard someone describe as 'the ugliest fruit with the prettiest smell'.

The body is what you'd expect from a Belgian-style wheat beer – a light, almost rice pudding sweetness and a pleasing roundness, but the joy is in the scent.

Gentleman's Wit is a citrus-laden delight for all the senses... in fact, it smells so pretty you could dab it behind your ears!

HITACHINO NEST WHITE ALE

ABV
5.5%

Country of origin
Japan

Try it if you like
Vodka and orange

Great with
Katsu curry

Also try
Moo Brew Hefeweizen
5%, Australia

Japan's craft beer scene is constantly changing. Previously more obsessed with imports than it was with its own breweries, that has slowly changed over the years and Hitachino has definitely been at the forefront of that.

I also have tremendous respect for how they feed and watered hundreds of people in the neighbourhood around them after the enormous tsunami and earthquake that hit the country in 2011, despite so much of their own brewery being affected.

Anyway, back to the beer. This ale has more spice than you'd normally expect from a Belgian-style beer, with nutmeg joining the traditional coriander (cilantro) and orange juice in addition to the expected peel, but all of it is done subtly, elevating this to more than just simple refreshment. It's a surprise with every sip.

SCHNEIDER WEISSE TAP 5 MEINE HOPFENWEISSE

ABV
8.2%

Country of origin
Germany

Try it if you like
Gin and tonic

Great with
Tandoori lamb cutlets

Also try
Cape Brewing Company
Krystal Weiss
5%, South Africa

It turns out that you can teach old dogs new tricks, as this beer proves!

This collaboration between the oldest commercial wheat beer brewery in Germany, Schneider Weisse, and relative whippersnappers Brooklyn Brewery - headed up by the legendary Garrett Oliver - was born out of a conversation between the two brewmasters about the relative merits of terroir in beer and led to the melding of the worlds of American craft beer and German brewing tradition and became a permanent fixture in the German brewery's line-up.

I think it's really cool that, despite his brewery being 400 years old, Georg VI Schneider wasn't against embracing ideas from the relatively young pups at Brooklyn in making a strong wheat beer that's hopped like an IPA – piney, grassy, resiny, but still intensely refreshing.

NAPARBIER HEFEWEIZEN

ABV
5.4%

Country of origin
Spain

Try it if you like
Gimlets

Great with
Crispy squid rings

Also try
Eisenbahn Weizenbier
4.8%, Brazil

Naparbier is one of the darlings of the Spanish beer scene and has gone from strength to strength in recent years.

This modern take on a German-style wheat beer includes the interesting Sorachi Ace* hop from Japan, which lends coconut and lemongrass notes and is underpinned by the lime-zest bitterness of the Citra hop used.

Not one for the purists, but then I'm not one of them, so I hope you enjoy it as much as I do!

*Sorachi Ace is the most divisive hop in the world! Some people smell coconut and lemongrass from it and others get a very strong sense of dill, whilst others - like me - find it smells like lemon furniture polish when used in excess or as a single hop.

3 FLOYDS GUMBALLHEAD

ABV
5.6%

Country of origin
USA

Try it if you like
Starburst®

Great with
Kielbasa with all the
trimmings

Also try
Brasserie Pietra Colomba
5%, France

I love 3 Floyds – they are anarchic, don't play by anyone's rules, are big on heavy metal and were once responsible for my husband finding me at 4 p.m. in the pub with them, toasting 'TO EVIL' and chasing pints with shots of Jameson... but anyway!

Just like the lovable hooligans who own the brewery, Gumballhead is a riotous romp of a beer that is all too easy to get into and just as likely to suddenly get you into trouble if you don't watch yourself.

Glorious tropical fruit flavours overlay a medium body, rounding off on a slightly sharp, sorbet-like finish. (Just don't follow it with a chaser of hard liquor and you should be fine!)

WAY BEER WITBIER

ABV
5.1%

Country of origin
Brazil

Try it if you like
Elderflower cordial

Great with
Pad Thai

Also try
Robson's Wheat Beer
5%, South Africa

This could be in the spice beer section (see pages 88–97), but the subtle use of all the botanicals persuaded me that it's better off here.

Based on a Belgian wheat beer recipe, it also uses Sicilian lemon peel, lemongrass and camomile – in chorus with the unique Sorachi Ace hop, which brings coconut to the party too.

Way is one of the most successful of the Brazilian craft brewers and with its striking paint splash branding and a growing number of awards, it is one to watch. (And I can't recommend their new fruited sour beers highly enough, perfect for the hot sunny Brazilian weather.)

ORANGE BEER ICE CREAM

**Makes about 1.5 litres
(52 fl oz) ice cream**

5 egg yolks

140 g (5 oz/⅔ cup) caster
(superfine) sugar or invertase
(whichever is cheaper!)

400 ml (13 fl oz/1½ cups) full-fat
(whole) milk (preferably
Jersey, which has extra fat
content that will make up for
the beer not having any)

75 ml (2½ fl oz/⅓ cup)
Belgian-style wheat beer

300 ml (10 fl oz/1¼ cups) double
(heavy) cream

zest of 2 oranges
(preferably blood orange,
if in season)

4 tablespoons orange juice
(partially frozen)

Beer ice cream? Why not? The beer brings a depth and freshness to it that really works and it's a delicious accompaniment to a chocolate torte or warm brownie.

Whisk together the yolks and sugar in a bowl until they're properly amalgamated and very pale.

Gently heat the milk, beer and cream in a saucepan until it starts to bubble. Gradually whisk into the egg yolk mixture. Do not stop whisking or you'll get lumps!

Pour the mixture back into the saucepan and heat really gently. Stir until thickened (I find one of those silicone spatulas is best for this). DO NOT STOP STIRRING.

When you can draw a firm line in the mixture using the back of the spatula you are done.

Stir in the orange zest and partially frozen orange juice, whisk briskly, leave to cool to room temperature, then place in the fridge to get very cold.

When cold and firm, pass the ice cream through a fine sieve, in case you scrambled some egg. Churn in an ice-cream maker until set. Store in an airtight container and keep in the freezer until ready to serve. Allow to defrost for a few minutes before scooping!

A SLY GIN

**Makes 2 of those big
Spanish goldfish bowls
(or big red wine glasses)**

ice cubes
50 ml (2 fl oz/¼ cup) simple syrup
·   infused with ginger and
    lemongrass*
70 ml (2½ fl oz/⅓ cup) gin
    (I use Sly Gin Lemon Verbena,
    but dry London is good too)
½ lemon, plus 2 peels from
    the skin
1 bottle of ice-cold Schneider
    Weisse Meine Hopfenweisse

You can make this much simpler and just have
Hopfenweisse and gin – honestly, it's great – but the
addition of ginger and lemongrass syrup is worthwhile.

Put some ice in the glasses to chill them. Shake more ice
and the syrup together for 30 seconds in a cocktail shaker.
Measure the gin into the shaker.

Squeeze the lemon in through your hand to catch the pips.
Add the beer and stir gently.

Empty the ice from the glasses and share the contents of
the shaker between the glasses. Garnish with a twist of
lemon peel.

* to make the simple syrup, add equal parts sugar and water to a
saucepan. Add in the bruised lemongrass and ginger and leave to
cool and infuse. It will keep, in a sealed jar, for a few weeks.

CHAPTER FOUR

HOP STARS

Hops are like the perfumes of the beer world; these little plants bring with them more than 250 identifiable aromas as well as bittering compounds and also bring anti-bacterial properties too, which means they are natural preservatives.

In fact, hops are pretty darn cool (and the closest known relative to cannabis, which is a good pub quiz fact). And it's in this chapter that we celebrate the best plant in the world, in my opinion, the plant that gives us aromas like rose, orange peel, grapefruit juice, Sauvignon Blanc, coconut, dill, lemongrass, key lime pie, cherry blossom, mango, lychee, pear and oh so much more.

In fact, you could say that this chapter is my love letter to Humulus lupulus and you wouldn't be far wrong.

SIERRA NEVADA TORPEDO EXTRA IPA

ABV
7.2%

Country of origin
USA

Try it if you like
Sierra Nevada Pale Ale

Great with
Slow-cooked lamb
shoulder

Also try
Pirate Life IPA
6.8%, Australia

No beer book would be complete without a mention of the truly pioneering and magnificent Sierra Nevada.

The brewery, or should I say breweries, as it now has two sites, is still family-owned and run and is estimated to be worth a whopping billion dollars.

But mere money can't put a price on its contribution to the resurrection of great beer the world over. From in-house childcare to a commitment to environmental consciousness, it is a business model to which all others should aspire.

Torpedo is a mainstay of the brewery's portfolio and, despite its weighty 7.2% ABV, is dangerously drinkable. Filled with pineappley, grapefruit notes and a chewy caramel body, it could easily sink you if you don't respect it, so do be careful!

MARBLE BREWERY DAMAGE PLAN

ABV
7.1%

Country of origin
UK

Try it if you like
Grapefruit juice

Great with
Seriously loud rock music

Also try
Devil's Peak King's
Blockhouse
6.7%, South Africa

James Kemp, affectionately known as JK, has been rocking out some seriously amazing beers since he hit the ground running at one of Britain's craft beer pioneers in 2016.

Marble Brewery has had a strong place in the hearts of UK beer lovers for the past 20 years, but has always been fairly parochial. However, his hiring was a clear signal by owner Jan Rogers that she was about to ramp up the brewery's presence both nationally and internationally.

Damage Plan has done exactly that. It's JK showing off how good he is at brewing easy-drinking big beers. (And it's also what I'm going to be rewarding myself with a can of, once I've finished this section!)

This big, bold homage to US West Coast-style IPAs is full of papaya, mango and pink grapefruit with a hint of fresh pine tips to it. As a cigar-smoking mercenary once said, 'I love it when a plan comes together.'

TEMPEST BREWING CO. LONG WHITE CLOUD

ABV
5.6%

Country of origin
New Zealand/UK

Try it if you like
New Zealand Sauvignon Blanc

Great with
Simply cooked scallops

Also try
Bieres Goutte d'Or Ernestine 7%, France

I've given this beer dual citizenship because it was born in a garage in Christchurch before migrating over to the UK for its graduation to a full commercial beer.

The brewery was founded by globe-trotting duo Gavin and Annika Meiklejohn, who met in Canada, conceived the idea for the brewery in New Zealand, and returned home to Gavin's native Scotland to make it happen.

Packed with New Zealand hops like Nelson Sauvin, Motueka, Waimea and Kohatu, Long White Cloud is one of the closest beers to a glass of New Zealand Sauvignon Blanc I've ever had. I could honestly just sit sniffing it for half an hour, it's so pretty!

Lychee, lime blossom, lemon zest, gooseberries and elderflower are all up front, and with its lightly creamy, almost spumante-like body and fresh finish, it is an all-time classic that I simply adore.

GREEN FLASH LE FREAK

ABV
9.2%

Country of origin
USA

Try it if you like
Orange marmalade

Great with
Gammon steaks

Also try
Baird Suruga Bay
Imperial IPA
8.5%, Japan

Green Flash is a San Diego icon and rightly so. Since it was founded in 2002 by Mike and Lisa Hinckley, it has pioneered different beer styles, this one being probably the most famous.

Using a Belgian yeast to make a heavily hopped Imperial IPA gives the beer an initial all over the map kind of aroma. First you smell a Belgian triple, then you get all the big Amarillo dry hop, and then you get that peppery spice that could be hops or the Belgian yeast – it's a conundrum that is as enticing as it is confusing.

But on the palate, all these elements come together in a glorious chorus of flavourful joy, as each one harmonises through the addition of a brioche-like malt profile that seamlessly connects each of the elements.

STONE & WOOD PACIFIC ALE

ABV
4.4%

Country of origin
Australia

Try it if you like
Peach compote

Great with
A Byron Bay bug

Also try
Oakham Citra
4.2%, UK

You know a beer is good if it can make it from one side of the world to the other and still taste stonkingly fresh, which is why Stone & Wood is in here.

Showcasing just one native hop, Galaxy, this billows with peach and apricot aromas and flavours and shines like early morning sun, with a slight haze from its lack of filtering.

And not only does the beer taste good, the brewery does good as well. Just like other environmentally and socially responsible businesses, such as New Belgium, Stone & Wood has set a very high standard for itself to tread lightly and leave only positive marks on the earth and its people – and I like that in a business.

BEAVERTOWN GAMMA RAY

ABV
5.4%

Country of origin
UK

Try it if you like
Tinned fruit salad

Great with
A classic cheeseburger

Also try
Bell's Two Hearted
7%, USA

One of my hometown favourites, Beavertown has been rocking it for five years now and shows no signs of abating. Founded by Logan Plant, the original site was in Duke's Brew & Que in Haggerston, East London, but the brewery quickly outgrew the restaurant site, moved to another venue for about a year and then finally broke ground on its current Tottenham home (which I'm slightly worried it may also have outgrown by the time this goes to press!).

One of the first London breweries to can its beers, decorated with striking artwork by creative director Nick Dwyer, Beavertown has been surfing the crest of the craft beer wave in the UK and I can't see it wiping out any time soon.

Gamma Ray is what the young whippersnappers round here call 'a juicy banger'; absolutely rammed full of tropical American hops, it reeks of mango and grapefruit and just a teeny bit of cattiness from the masses of Columbus, Bravo, Amarillo, Citra and Calypso, and is a beer I often use to zap away a bad day at the office.

TWO BIRDS
BANTAM IPA

ABV
4.7%

Country of origin
Australia

Try it if you like
Long Island Ice Tea

Great with
Steak

Also try
Minoh W-IPA
9%, Japan

I've been following the story of these plucky ladies from early on and I was thrilled when they finally got their bricks and mortar brewery in 2014 and have seen them go from strength to strength.

The two women at the helm, Jayne Lewis and Danielle Allen, have actually known each other since childhood but didn't realise quite how much until they embarked on two-week road trip along the US West Coast and their idea for a beer business emerged.

Two Birds is an obvious play on the Aussie (and British) nick name for a woman but they have made it more than that, with their nest firmly established they are kicking arse and taking names - as they should. Bantam is my personal favourite of theirs, a full-bodied IPA that shows restraint in both its alcohol content and its bitterness, whilst not stinting on its tropical aromas and pithy finish. In fact, this beer, like its namesake, punches well above its weight.

MAGIC ROCK INHALER

ABV
4.5%

Country of origin
UK

Try it if you like
Fruit salad

Great with
Strawberry shortcake

Also try
Sainte Cru Tempete
du Desert
5.5%, France

·Magic Rock has quickly established itself as one of the cool kids of the UK brewing scene, but managed to do so without shouting and screaming, which is nice.

Based in Huddersfield in Yorkshire, the brewery has grown very quickly and has one of the most impressive set-ups in the country, including a very cool taproom.

Inhaler is somewhere between a pale ale and an IPA. I dithered for a long time between including this and Human Cannonball, which also got lots of love from people. But I have chosen this one because it's so elegant and Human Cannonball is a little less accessible.

I also like that some of the juiciness of this beer comes from the selection of malts. The Crystal T50 gives a slight golden raisin note to the beer that just tones down all the booming fruit a little and pulls it together with a whisper of honey.

IPA AND GRAPEFRUIT VINAIGRETTE

50 ml (2 fl oz/¼ cup) honey mustard

50 ml (2 fl oz/¼ cup) grapefruit juice

50 ml (2 fl oz/¼ cup) citrus IPA

1 teaspoon caster (superfine) sugar

250 ml (8½ fl oz/1 cup) groundnut (peanut) or grapeseed oil (or very light olive oil, but not extra virgin, it's too bitter)

1 egg yolk, per 500 ml (17 fl oz/ 2 cups) dressing

sea salt and freshly ground black pepper, to taste

This is a really simple dressing that work very well with a variety of different salads but my personal favourite is to put it with a warm grain-based salad like tabbouleh with some lightly poached fish or salty halloumi.

Put all the ingredients into an old, clean jar, tighten the lid very well* and shake until emulsified.

*I'm always prescriptive about putting the lid very tightly on salad dressing before shaking it; when I was a kid we had what is referred to as 'The Thousand Island Dressing Incident' where my dad forgot to check the lid on a bottle of said dressing and we were still finding blobs of it on the top of kitchen cupboards and other random areas of the room three years later.

CHAPTER FIVE

RED,
AMBER
AND
BROWN

Poor brown beer, it gets such a bad rep. Nasty people call it 'twiggy beer' or 'old man's beer' or 'warm, flat beer' – they just don't appreciate its subtleties, so I've decided it needs a little bit of love, before we start, so, here we go: 'I'm Melissa, and I love brown beer'. There, I said it!

I love a satisfying English bitter, with a bready, nutty body, a lightly hay-like astringent middle and that balanced, lightly bitter but oh-so-moreish finish – I can honestly say that one of my most transcendent beer experiences was trying Bathams Best Bitter from cask for the first time.

But this chapter isn't all about bitters; I also enjoy a big, berry and citrus laden imperial red ale, stuffed to the gunwales with booming American hops and a drop kick of bitterness at the end, like one of my favourites Bear Republic's Racer 5. But I can also want somewhere in between, maybe an amber ale with that refreshing quality of a bitter but with some of that brash hop character that IPA lovers lust after - like Wiper & True's Amber ale. Hopefully this intro has whet your appetite to cast your net wider across this often neglected spectrum of beers (and yes, I have snuck three more recommendations in here because I really like these styles and I ran out of room for some of my favourites!).

MOOR RAW

ABV
4.3%

Country of origin
UK

Try it if you like
An after-work refresher

Great with
Cold roast beef sandwich

Also try
Victory Brewing Uncle Teddy's British Bitter 3.9%, UK

It amuses me somewhat that one of the best bitters in the UK is made by a Californian. Justin Hawke first came to my attention years ago when he had a brewery in the back end of nowhere. Having plied his trade in the US prior to moving to the UK he was pretty uncomfortable with the idea of finings in beer (clarifying agents that can be, but aren't limited to, a fish by-product) and was perfectly comfortable with a bit of haze in the beer - which is more than can be said of the British drinkers of the time.

However, Hawke's persistence and a growing number of other brewers (including Fuller's, which has, at the time of writing, released an unfiltered version of London Pride in keg) that also hold the same view, are slowly helping to change that attitude and it's all for the betterment of beer in general, because the less messed about beer is after it is made, the more flavour it has.

Anyway, back to Raw, which is a joy to quaff: dry, bready, a little herbal, with a tad of orange chocolate in the background, and is best drunk in great big gulps after a long day at work.

THE WALL BREWERY SJAVÁR BJÓR

ABV
5.2%

Country of origin
Italy

Try it if you like
Salted caramel

Great with
Pork and 'nduja
meatballs

Also try
Little Creatures Rogers'
3.8%, Australia

The Italian beer scene is, for me, the most improved of anywhere in the world in the last three years. Holding so much promise for so long, with a handful of producers making exceptional beer, it failed to reach the heady heights of even a hundred excellent breweries nationwide until just recently.

The Wall initially collaborated on this beer with Birrificio Argo, a small brewery that also makes a very good American amber called Amberground, but the production has moved permanently to The Wall, as it is the larger of the two.

Based on the idea of, rather than a literal translation of, salt caramel, it's one of those beers that grows on you. The addition of sea salt right before packaging elevates the caramel notes in the malt body of the beer, makes the subtle hops a little brighter, and overall has that effect of making you reach for your glass a little quicker than you normally would!

ANSPACH & HOBDAY THE SMOKED BROWN

ABV
6%

Country of origin
UK

Try it if you like
Smoky whiskies

Great with
Vegetable, chickpea
and harissa tagine

Also try
Aecht Schlenkerla
Rauchbier Märzen
5.1%, Germany

Anspach & Hobday are real people. Yes, I know it sounds like something a US TV series would call a pair of Victorian detectives but, honestly, they are two lovely lads, with a very serious work ethic and a very bijoux brewery.

The Smoked Brown is a beer that they took a long time to perfect, as they wanted to nod towards the traditions of traditional Bamberg Rauch beers but at the same time make something with a British soul.

Aged on oak chips, it has a charming and witty complexity that sneaks up on you with its depth. It is not overwhelmingly phenolic (the fancy way to describe antiseptic smells and tastes), but has more subtle and rounded smoky notes, with chocolate, caramel and a hint of espresso woven into it.

HACKNEY
RED

ABV
4.1%

Country of origin
UK

Try it if you like
Light red wines

Great with
Sweet and sour tofu

Also try
Terrapin Rye Pale Ale
5.4%, USA

Hackney Brewery was one of the first wave of inhabitants in East London's once again legendary brewing scene. Quietly going about its business with an office full of dogs and a warm welcome always on hand, it's a brewery I don't think gets enough plaudits.

The red took a while to make its mark, having been introduced early in the brewery's history. It didn't seem to sell and disappeared for a few years before being brought back – and I couldn't be happier.

Rich malt loaf flavours are overlaid by fruity, floral American hops like Chinook and Centennial to create a glamorously garnet-hued glass of gorgeousness, that tastes more complex than its 4.1% alcohol strength would suggest.

BAGBY BEER THREE BEAGLES BROWN

ABV
5.6%

Country of origin
USA

Try it if you like
English milds

Great with
A classic hot dog

Also try
AleSmith Nut Brown Ale
5%, USA

Co-owner and brewer Jeff Bagby has an intrinsic understanding of how to make UK-style beers like few other US brewers I've met, balancing satisfying flavours with subtle complexity, and he is just one of the amazing people I was introduced to by my late, great friend Glenn Payne, to whom this book is dedicated.

Jeff and his business partner wife Dande named Three Beagles after their love of the breed and it is a lovely dry, easy-drinking brown ale with hints of toffee, dark chocolate and berry fruit, and a little suggestion of orange liqueur.

But be careful: it's one of those beers that only lets you know how strong it is about halfway down the third pint!

TEXELS BOCK

ABV
7%

Country of origin
Netherlands

Try it if you like
Oloroso sherry

Great with
Smoked ham hock
and mash

Also try
Ayinger Celebrator
Doppelbock
6.7%, Germany

On an island off the north of the Netherlands is a population that is outnumbered by sheep about three to one but, amazingly, its brewery is about to open a second site dedicated to brewing its flagship beer - that's a success story if I ever heard one.

And Texels brewery is all about passion, from its man-mountain ambassador Hans Glandorf who lives, breathes and bellows the brand, to how they source their ingredients to supporting the local economy.

Although Bock is technically a lager, it has more in common with a strong ale on the palate, with its richness. The first thing you'll notice is the striking deep amber with garnet highlights, so it's worth popping in a big red wine glass to truly admire it. Then the nose hits you, big boozy raisiny, pruney Olorosso sherry notes interwoven with some orange peel and a brisk carbonation that make it both complex and dangerously drinkable at the same time.

It's also worth noting that the Dutch Bock Bier festival in Amsterdam is the largest beer fest in the whole of Europe, dedicated to just one style... got to love those crazy Dutch!

ISE KADOYA BROWN ALE

ABV
5%

Country of origin
Japan

Try it if you like
IPAs

Great with
Sweet potato korokke

Also try
Harvey's Sussex Best
Bitter
4%, UK

It's an unfortunate truth that when you judge beers, you always come at it from a fairly depressing standpoint: because you start by looking for faults and then you go from there.

But sometimes, a beer crosses your table that stops you in your tracks and you almost forget that you're not supposed to just sit and enjoy drinking it!

When I judged this beer it sang to me immediately. A smooth, caramel body is overlaid with a hint of rose, aromatic heather, pine and a pop of grapefruit, making it like enjoying an elegant US-style IPA, but with a body on steroids. Also unusually for a lot of Japanese beers, it stands up extremely well to travelling.

SKA BREWING PINSTRIPE RED ALE

ABV
5.2%

Country of origin
USA

Try it if you like
Blackcurrants

Great with
Croque madame

Also try
Anchor Steam Beer
4.9%, USA

There is something in the air in Colorado that makes so many of them such damn good brewers - seriously, I don't know if it's the Rockies, or that so many of them are nearly 7ft tall but there's something going on in that State that seems to lend itself to great beer and Ska is no exception.

Run by joyfully anarchic characters it is, nonetheless, very serious about its beer, in a rather irreverent way and whilst I disagree with the brewery's characterisation of a 5.2% beer being 'sessionable', I don't disagree that it's brilliant, so that's why it's here!

A soothing caramel base is very simply overlaid with Liberty hops, which bring a tinkly blackcurrant, some rich lily-like notes and a nice, nettly spice that brings everything to a sweeping crescendo at the finish.

NORTH END BREWING AMBER

ABV
4.4%

Country of origin
New Zealand

Try it if you like
Marmalade

Great with
Spicy pork ribs

Also try
Jopen Jacobus RPA
5.5%, Netherlands

Brewer Kieran Haslett-Moore is a man with a serious passion for beer. Formerly a beer buyer for an off-licence chain, he has successfully done what few do, switched sides, and has been gaining fans ever since.

I had the pleasure of a collaborative brew day with Kieran. Amber was a beer that was drunk a fair bit while we used foraged ingredients from his late grandfather's lands, shot the breeze about our ethos around beer and generally had a great day.

The reason the Amber was a beer we returned to was its easy-drinking nature, which just allowed conversation to flow (and was also particularly satisfying after digging out the mash tun!)

Taking influences from both US and UK bitter styles, it is still a uniquely New Zealand beer due to the hops used. It contains beautifully integrated caramelised marmalade and rye bread hints, with a suggestion of thyme and lime zest, and is deeply refreshing.

SIMPLE
BEER
BREAD

**Makes 1 loaf
(23 cm × 13 cm/5 in × 9 in)**

For the dry ingredients
300 g (10½ oz/2 cups)
    strong wholemeal flour
200 g (7 oz/1⅓ cups)
    strong white flour
1 teaspoon fine sea salt
1 teaspoon dried yeast

For the wet ingredients
1½ teaspoons maple syrup
150 ml (5 fl oz/⅔ cup)
    boiling water
150 ml (5 fl oz/⅔ cup)
    sweet brown ale
    (or Dunkelweizen)
1½ teaspoons groundnut
    (peanut) oil (or another
    fairly neutral oil)

You can use a stand mixer or your hands for this. Either is fine – the timings are all the same. You'll need a ½ pint (285 ml/9 fl oz) of tap water to hand for the baking part.

Put all the dry ingredients in a bowl or mixer and mix together quickly.

Add the maple syrup to the boiling water and stir until dissolved, then add the cold beer. This should give you the perfect temperature to add to the dough.

Stir half the liquid into the dry ingredients, then continue to add smaller amounts until a dough forms. You may not need all of it, you may need a bit more – every flour is different! Knead for about 8–10 minutes until smooth. Turn out into a lightly oiled bowl, cover with a damp tea towel and leave somewhere at 26°C (80°F) for 30–35 minutes.

Preheat the oven to 210°C (410°F/Gas 6–7).

Knock back the dough and leave to rise again for another 15–20 minutes. Gently turn the dough out into a lightly oiled loaf tin and get ready to move quickly!

Put the bread tin within grabbing distance and pick up the glass of tap water (see intro above). Open the oven door and throw the water on the base of the oven, grab the tin and put it on the middle shelf and close the door as quickly as possible – this helps form a good crust on your loaf.

Check the loaf for even browning after about 25 minutes and turn it if necessary. It should be done in about 40 minutes total.

Leave for at least 10 minutes. I know it's torture, but that just completes the final bit of cooking in the middle and means you won't get a tummy ache!

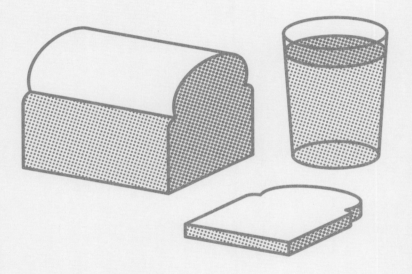

CHAPTER SIX

SPICE UP YOUR LIFE

This is where my two great gustatory loves cross over – cooking and brewing.

Historically, in regions where hops weren't grown or really understood, beers would have been brewed with the addition of any herb, spice or botanical that was to hand.

Often these would have been slightly bitter to offset the intrinsic sweetness of the beer itself, and included things like bog myrtle, yarrow, alecost, heather, juniper and pretty much anything else that smelled like it would taste good!

So, in this section I've chosen beers that use herbs or spices, or unusual ingredients such as seaweed, to create beers with excellent drinkability and intrigue – not just those that stampede through your palate like a herd of angry hippos.

BRASSERIE DU MONT BLANC LA BLONDE

ABV
5.8%

Country of origin
France

Try it if you like
Belgian blonde ales

Great with
Tartiflette

Also try
Savour Saison
5%, UK

Brasserie du Mont Blanc is a story of resurrection. In 1996 the original business, which was formed in 1821, ceased trading and it was down to local lad Sylvain Chiron to step in and resurrect its fortunes.

While studying in the US, Chiron was taken with the explosion of microbreweries. Back in France, he worked with a Cistercian abbey to produce liqueurs. When he returned to Savoy and discovered that the brewery had shut down, he decided to revive it.

With a little help from another monastery in Belgium, he learned the art of brewing and then discovered a mountain stream that would become the source of his beer. The influence from his liqueur and syrup making days is clear in his regular use of spices. In the case of La Blonde, it's liquorice root that adds a slight savoury edge to the beer, stopping it from becoming another one-dimensional blonde beer.

The other key step is that the beer is lagered for around four weeks, giving it a clean crispness. Mind you, Mont Blanc is the perfect location to keep it cold!

YEASTIE BOYS GUNNAMATTA

ABV
6.5%

Country of origin
New Zealand

Try it if you like
Earl Grey tea

Great with
Cucumber sandwiches

Also try
Siren Yulu
3.6%, UK

*Cuckoo brewers,
also known as gypsy
brewers, are beer makers
who use spare capacity
in other breweries.
Contract brands give
their recipe to a brewery
and get them to make it
for them.

I first encountered the deliciously mad Stu McKinlay and Sam Possenniskie when they landed at Heathrow from New Zealand and came straight to a beer festival called Craft Beer Rising. With a suitcase full of plastic bottles of their beer, they proceeded to rock a tasting that I was hosting by being part-jet lagged, part-tipsy and all themselves. Stu has now relocated to the UK permanently as it's such an important market to them. They are cuckoo brewers*, but they always keep a beady eye on the quality of their beer.

Gunnamatta was one of their first flagship beers and remains a firm favourite. Using high-quality blue leaf Earl Grey tea is one of the keys to its incredibly fragrant and attractive bergamot aroma, which they describe as smelling 'much like your granny's bedroom'. Not a sales pitch to me personally as my grandmother smoked 40 a day, but I can see what they're getting at!

Regardless, it's a great concept to bring together a modern IPA, with those distinctive citrus and floral New Zealand hop notes, and a very traditional ingredient to create what can best be described as a boozy, beery iced tea.

CEVEJA MORADA HOP ARABICA

ABV
5%

Country of origin
Brazil

Try it if you like
Cold brew coffee

Great with
Pastel de nata

Also try
Standeaven
Watermelon Lager
4.7%, South Africa

In the town Curitiba in Brazil is a whole host of brewers, I'm not sure why it has become such a conurbation for beer makers but it has, with cuckoo and contract brewers aplenty.

Maybe it's the slightly more temperate climate than much of the rest of the country that makes it slightly more bearable to brew in, I don't know, but whatever it is, it is turning out some belting beers. And one of these cuckoo breweries is Cerveja Morada, run by some of the loveliest, most hospitable people I've ever met. Andre Junqueira, along with wife and Fernanda Lazarri, has been home brewing for years before taking the step to launching a commercial brand and it's clearly paid off as the beers are brilliant.

The one that stands out to me however, is the Hop Arabica. Made in collaboration with Lucca Cafés Especiais de Curitiba, it is an unusual coffee beer in that it is pale. In the same way that cold brew is known, but rare, as are pale coffee beers but this is a work of sheer genius in my opinion. The super-fruity coffee is integrated to the light, fruity hops used with a mega-refreshing end and a light acidity and bitterness that peaks the palate into wanting more.

WILLIAMS BROS. KELPIE

ABV
4.4%

Country of origin
UK

Try it if you like
Dark beers

Great with
Truffled macaroni cheese

Also try
Ramses Bier Naar De
Haenen
5%, Netherlands
(collaboration with
Stadsbrouwerij de
Pilgrim)

The Williams Bros. are among the founders of the UK craft brewing movement and one of the most dominant players in Scotland for the last 20 years.

They started off as a home brew shop in Glasgow but one day a lady came in with a historic recipe for heather ale and changed the course of Bruce and Scott Williams' lives. 'Leanne Fraoch' was the title of the recipe, later shortened to just Fraoch, and it soon became the brewery's flagship beer. It was joined by other historic ales and, when they moved into their current brewery in Alloa, contemporary brews as well.

Kelpie is the outlier in the 'historic ales' family at Williams. It isn't really a historic recipe per se, it's more an attempt to recreate the flavour of the long-gone Scottish coastal ale houses, which would have used the unique coastal barley that adds a slight flavour of the sea.

Today, the brewery adds seaweed to this beer that, initially, tastes like a very pleasant chocolatey, dark porter... but that's because you haven't noticed the seaweed's umami, which makes the beer incredibly moreish and has you craving another in short order!

TWO CHEFS BREWING WHITE MAMBA

ABV
5%

Country of origin
Netherlands

Try it if you like
Thai flavours

Great with
Charcuterie

Also try
Seasons Basilicow
5%, Brazil

You have to love the crazy Dutch, and Two Chefs are definitely right up there. The brewery was founded, unsurprisingly, by two guys who had been chefs and then entered corporate life. In 2012, they chucked in their suits, decided to re-join the creative world and haven't looked back.

Although they started off cuckoo brewing, the pair and their ever-expanding team decided they needed their own brewery and started a crowdfunding campaign in 2016, managing to raise €300,000 in just six weeks. They now have a big, new, shiny home in the northwest of Amsterdam and the beers have taken a big leap forward in consistency.

A lot of the brews have a culinary bent to them but White Mamba, for me, stands out as the most interesting, with coriander seeds, lemongrass and cardamom used throughout the process, but all very subtly, giving it a really refreshing character with significantly less bite than its namesake!

It's also worth trying Tropical Ralphie, named after Two Chefs' irrepressible first employee and wonderfully hyperactive ambassador.

CALAVERA MEXICAN IMPERIAL STOUT

ABV
9%

Country of origin
Mexico

Try it if you like
Mole

Great with
Chocolate ice cream

Also try
Rogue Sriracha Hot
Stout Beer
5.7%, USA

Owned by Elizabeth Rosas González and husband Gilbert Nielsen, Calavera is one of a new wave of Mexican brewers with a woman at the helm. It can be a struggle in a country where beer drinkers and buyers are mostly men, but that's not stopping them. González and Nielsen caught the bug of home brewing whilst in Denmark and founded the brewery in Tlalnepantla.

I might have started this section by denouncing stampeding chilli beers, but there is a good reason for that. There's so much hyper-macho posturing around making chilli beers incredibly hot that I find a lot of them undrinkable.

However, even though this beer does pack a decent punch, it is tempered and rounded by a blend of chillies and the background sweetness of the beer style, with its rich chocolate and coffee notes, and not exacerbated by the use of really aggressive hops.

PROPER CORNED BEEF

Serves 4–6

450 g (1 lb) Cornish sea salt
25 g (1 oz) pink curing salt
2.5 kg (5½ lb) brisket
4 smoked garlic cloves, smashed
3 bottles of chilled Kelpie
    (or other low-hop herb beer)
1 tablespoon bourbon

For the pickling spice
1 teaspoon allspice berries
4 teaspoons black peppercorns
1 teaspoon white peppercorns
4 teaspoons black mustard seeds
5 teaspoons coriander seeds
2 cascabel chillies,
    deseeded and torn
1½ teaspoons blade mace
1 small cinnamon stick
20 dried bay leaves, crumbled
½ teaspoon whole cloves
1 teaspoon ground ginger
2 teaspoons dill seeds
1 teaspoon fennel seeds
1 teaspoon celery seeds
½ teaspoon seaweed (such as
    wakame, laverbread or nori)

This is a big recipe so you can halve it, but it is easier to make the full amount of pickling spice. It can be stored for at least 2 months in an airtight container or, of course, used to make pickles.

Don't forget, though, if you are able to make the big bit of brisket, you can turn half of it into pastrami... mmmm, pastrami...

To make the pickling spice, simply dry fry the spices, adding the bigger, more robust ones like the allspice first and the more delicate ones like the dill seeds later.

To brine the meat, warm up 4 litres (8½ pints) of water and add the salts, stirring until dissolved. Take off the heat and throw in 3 tablespoons of the pickling spice and the garlic cloves, then add 2 bottles of the chilled beer (which'll help bring the temperature down quicker).

Pour the brine into a non-metallic tub or sealable bag (ziplock or vacuum is fine), then add the brisket and chill for 5–7 days (no longer or it gets too salty).

When you are ready to cook the brisket, wash the brisket to clean it of the pickling spices and place it in a large pan of cold water. Bring it to the boil, then discard the water.

Add the remaining bottle of beer and the bourbon to the pan and top up with water. Pop in 3 tablespoons of the pickling spice in a muslin bag. Cook very low and slow (keep it 85–95°C/185–200°F) with bubbles just breaking the surface for 5–6 hours or until very tender.

MY THAI

Serves 1

1 teaspoon sugar
1 fresh kaffir lime leaf
2 teaspoons ginger liqueur
   (I use King's Ginger)
50 ml (2 fl oz/¼ cup) vodka
   (you could use chilli vodka,
   preferably home-made)
juice of ½ lime
330 ml (11 fl oz/1⅓ cups)
   cold Thai-flavoured beer
   such as Two Chefs White
   Mamba

This is my version of the classic fave Mai Tai and is a really fun way to introduce beer to friends who may not necessarily drink it. In fact, I'd even go so far as to say this is just silly fun but, in my opinion, that's never a bad thing to embrace in life!

In a shaker, muddle the sugar and the lime leaf together until you can really smell the aromatics, then put in a shaker with some ice and all the other ingredients apart from the beer and shake for 30 seconds.

Strain into a tall glass and top up with the beer.

CHAPTER SEVEN

FRUIT BEERS

First things first, fruit beers don't have to be sweet - in fact I have a confession to make here, I don't have much of a sweet tooth (unless it's pick 'n' mix and then I shouldn't be allowed to handle one of those scoops unattended).

So this chapter is a real mixture; there are some traditional fruit beers that span back over centuries, there are some great fun beers where the brewer has let loose their inner child in the candy store and there are some serious beers too (but not too serious because, after all, that's not what beer is about).

All in all I'd like you to put aside any potential prejudices against fruit beers and give them another go (this is also where I wish that there was a pea beer, so I could ask you to give peas a chance, but no one has made one yet, so I'll just have to keep that terrible dad joke for another day).

OUD BEERSEL OUDE KRIEK

ABV
6.5%

Country of origin
Belgium

Try it if you like
Cherry pie

Great with
Ale roast duck

Also try
Funkwerks Raspberry
Provision
4.2%, USA

Choosing a traditional Belgian brewer for this section was incredibly tough, so I'm going to start this bit by saying if you like this try more – try Tilquin, Boon, Duchesse de Bourgogne, 3 Fonteinen, Lindemans, Cantillon, Petrus and Rodenbach – because these are the guardians of a unique and wonderful style of beer.

Anyway, back to Oud Beersel. Founded in 1882, the brewery fell into financial troubles in 2002, but in 2005 it was rescued by two friends, Gert Christiaens and Roland De Bus. Inheriting an aluminium brew kit (not advisable at all), they had to outsource the actual making of the beer to Frank Boon.

The good news is that there will soon be a brewery back up and running at Oud Beersel and the beers, which have remained barrel-aged and blended on site, are sensational. This is my favourite of them all – brisk, complex, leathery, almondy, like a tart cherry pie, which can be explained by the fact that there is at least 400 g (14 oz) of cherries used for each litre (34 fl oz) of beer. The brewery has plans to plant an orchard so that they can source their cherries as locally as possible.

21ST AMENDMENT HELL OR HIGH WATERMELON

ABV
4.9%

Country of origin
USA

Try it if you like
Watermelon

Great with
The beach

Also try
Captain Lawrence
Brewing Effortless
Grapefruit IPA
4.5%, USA

I can't write this section and leave out one of my favourite beers in the world from a brewery that I adore. 21st Amendment, headed up by Nico Freccia and Shaun 'Sully' O'Sullivan, is a San Francisco-based icon and their brewpub is well worth a visit.

Hell or High is a subtle and graceful beer, but I've got be honest, when my dear friend Richard Dinwoodie first told me about it I had some serious reservations, as he's got the sweetest tooth of anyone I know. But when I drank it for the first time at the Great American Beer Festival, I couldn't keep a big silly grin off my face – I'd found watermelon nirvana.

The sweet wheat body of the beer, with just a hint of slickness, lightly weaves in and out of the pure watermelon taste. It's not at all candy-like; it just reminds me of eating lumps of watermelon with my sister on a hot beach in Corfu when I was a kid, spitting the seeds into the water and watching the fish rush to them, and then jumping into the azure sea to wash off all the sticky watermelon juice.

Any beer that gives you that feeling is a gift and one I thank the brewing deities for.

WICKED WEED GENESIS

ABV
6.6%

Country of origin
USA

Try it if you like
Tropical fruit salad

Great with
BBQ jerk fish

Also try
2Cabeças/Cevejaria
Dadiva Pink Lemonade
4.4%, Brazil

Feel the fruity funk with Wicked Weed's fabulous barrel-aged Genesis. The very first beer that took this brewery from home brew to professional, it has undergone some changes over time, but remains a firm fan favourite.

Made with a huge amount of papaya, guava, mango and pineapple, this Belgian-style blonde ale is then aged for six to 12 months in white wine barrels, where the wild yeast and other bacterial beasts do their thing to make this a fruity delight of epic proportions.

An explosion of pineapple on the nose, a dry papaya and guava middle and a rich crescendo of mango and crystallised pineapple on the edge are all joined by a bit of Brett earthiness and a satisfying zip and zing of yoghurt sourness.

I think of this beer as something to drink with a big bloom tucked behind your ear, following the faint smell of barbecue down the beach somewhere tropical, with the faint strains of steel drums in the distance.

THORNBRIDGE & ST ERIK'S IMPERIAL RASPBERRY STOUT

ABV
10%

Country of origin
UK/Sweden

Try it if you like
Dark chocolate

Great with
Loin of venison

Also try
Unibroue Éphémère
5.5%, Canada

Thornbridge Brewery is arguably one of the most successful craft breweries in the UK and has a long-standing reputation for its flagship beer Jaipur, which by my reckoning is the most highly awarded beer in the UK. But, for me, this stout is something really special, which may be helped by the fact that the woman who collaborated with Thornbridge, Jessica Heidrich, is also my roomie when we are judging at festivals in the USA.

Jessica is a pioneer in the Swedish beer industry, the modern era's first female brewmaster and a seriously smart lady. She is someone I very much look up to in the beer world.

The beer, just like Jessica, is poised, intelligent and elegant. The dark chocolate and coffee malt base is carefully teased to the softer side by the use of pounds and pounds of Scottish raspberries, which are considered the best in the world by food lovers.

As a result, the beer is anything but saccharine. It's rich, complex and just boozy enough to give your cheeks a little glow – a very grown-up drink indeed.

BRASSERIE ST GERMAIN & NØGNE Ø RHUB'IPA

ABV
6%

Country of origin
France/Norway

Try it if you like
Rhubarb

Great with
Mackerel

Also try
Young Henrys Mulberia
4%, USA

I love rhubarb and I love that, in the UK, there is a place called the rhubarb triangle in Yorkshire that specialises in producing that vibrant pink forced rhubarb you see in the early months of the year. I also love the beer I've made with it called Siberia – but, much as it pains me, I have to admit I think this one is better.

This collaboration between two great brewers, Brasserie St Germain and Nøgne Ø, is every beery rhubarb-lover's dream – made with 10% rhubarb juice and tropical New Zealand hops, it is a fruity riot without being too sweet.

And please don't ask me how to pronounce Nøgne Ø. Every time I think I've nailed it, I get told I'm wrong. It would appear that the Nordic languages just aren't for me!

8 WIRED FEIJOA

ABV
Various

Country of origin
New Zealand

Try it if you like
Bazooka Joe bubblegum

Great with
A confused expression

Also try
Cantillon Lou Pepe Kriek
5%, Belgium

If you are ever in New Zealand, don't ask what a Feijoa is in front of a group of natives. If my experience of doing so at 8 Wired's brewery is anything to go by, it's like saying you don't know that the sky is blue or water is wet.

Don't ask what Feijoa tastes like, either. No single person will give you the same answer, but 20 different folk will spend a good 10 minutes giving you their version. This must be because they don't sell Bazooka Joe bubblegum down there and that's EXACTLY what it tastes like (well, to me anyway).

This beer is a glorious romp through the culinary unknown for most people, but it's a fun one nonetheless. The beer is brewed as a fairly simple pale ale, then poured into different barrels, which are impregnated with various wild yeasts and bacteria and left to age for about a year before the lunatics at 8 Wired shove 800 kg (1750 lb) of fruit through the barrels' bung holes (around 30 in total). They are then sealed up for around another year to pick up all the fruit's flavour.

The end result is like sour gum balls in beer form, and who couldn't be happy with that?

TINGLY OYSTERS

Serves 4 (3 oysters each)

12 fresh oysters
4 teaspoons red wine vinegar
½ tablespoon finely minced shallot
1 teaspoon freshly grated
    horseradish, pounded to a paste
    in a pestle and mortar
1½ tablespoons Oud Beersel or
    other sharp Kriek beer, well
    chilled

The last minute addition of beer to this classic oyster accompaniment brings a little added frisson to it. It makes me giggle every time I eat it because it literally tickles the tastebuds!

Shuck the oysters (carefully) and arrange on a serving plate, as you want to get this to the table as quickly as possible.

Prepare all the ingredients and mix everything together thoroughly apart from the beer (keep that until the last minute).

When you are ready to serve, mix in the beer and get it to the table as quickly as you can to preserve the light effervescence of the beer – that way you can enjoy the tingly oysters! Enjoy with the rest of the beer, served in champagne flutes.

RUBE ICON

Serves 1

50 ml (2 fl oz/¼ cup) lychee liqueur
2 teaspoons lime juice
150 ml (5 fl oz/⅔ cup) tropical
  fruit-flavoured beer (preferably
  sour, or add 1 tablespoon
  triple sec)

Another terrible play on words, this is a boozy version
of the tropical drink Rubicon, which was a feature of my
childhood. I'm sure all over the world there are tropical
punch-flavoured drinks that you'll identify as similar.

Shake the lychee liqueur and the lime juice together over
ice and strain into a martini glass. Top up with beer, stir
gently and serve.

CHAPTER EIGHT

FARMHOUSE BEERS

Farmhouse beers really means most beers that were brewed before the industrialisation of the process. Chucking fermentable ingredients in a pot and boiling them up to make booze is pretty much as old as upright mankind, but in the beer world it mainly refers to the Belgian and French styles of farmhouse brewing.

The main difference between the French style of farmhouse ale, known as Bière de Garde, and the Belgian, known as Saison, is the ABV and the different characteristics of the yeast strains.

Bières de Garde tend to be stronger and akin to a blonde ale, while Saisons tend to be drier and leaner and have a more peppery, spicy character, but they do have something in common in that they were working-class drinks. Made mainly for migrant farm hands, they were often the result of whatever leftover crops were fermentable, then left to age until the next harvest.

Because no one knows a huge amount about these styles, they have become increasingly difficult to define. Purists insist they should have some sourness to them, while others point out that, as brewing technology has moved on, so has the need for sourness. I'm sure that you don't give a hoot about this argument and just want me to tell you the best beers, so I shall crack on.

BOULEVARD TANK 7

ABV
8.5%

Country of origin
USA

Try it if you like
Dry Riesling

Great with
Taleggio cheese

Also try
Brew by Numbers
Motueka & Lime
5.5%, UK

Oh Tank 7, how do I love thee, let me count the ways! Yeah, I know, it's a bit melodramatic, but I really, really like this beer.

Creator and head brewer at Boulevard, Steven Pauwels, brought all his know-how from his native Belgium and applied it to the American brew scene to create this fruity, bone-dry delight.

Named after the tank that it is aged in, which had for some reason caused them headaches for every other beer they'd tried to brew in it, the beer has rapidly become a benchmark for all other modern Saisons.

On the nose it has hints of dried orange peel and red apple with touches of white pepper, then an earthy body is joined by a dash of pink grapefruit at the end and a deliciously astringent finish that leaves the mouth begging for more.

BURNING SKY SAISON À LA PROVISION

ABV
6.5%

Country of origin
UK

Try it if you like
Fino sherry

Great with
Smoked cheese

Also try
Crooked Stave Surrette
Provision Saison
6.2%, USA

When Mark Tranter announced he was leaving Dark Star and starting his own brewery, the whole UK beer scene sat up and took notice. He walked me round the place where he was hoping to build, and it's one of the toughest things I've ever been sworn to secrecy on. I wanted to shout from the rooftops that this was going to be something special.

And special it is. While waiting for planning permission, Mark went on a whirlwind odyssey, visiting some of the best brewers of farmhouse ales, from Colorado to Belgium. Armed with tips, he came back and opened Burning Sky and neither he nor his fans have ever looked back. Although he doesn't focus solely on Saisons – he also makes some fantastic session beers and IPAs – you can see in his eyes that the fouders in his brewery are his biggest love.

Saison à la Provision is brewed with Mark's purist hat on. A traditionally hopped wort is first fermented with a saison yeast and then treated to a dose of Brett and lactobacillus for a dry, tart finish to the straw-like, bready body with a hint of marigold. If I were a farm worker given this at the end of a long hard day, I'd probably kiss my employer there and then!

BRASSERIE DUYCK JENLAIN AMBRÉE

ABV
7.5%

Country of origin
France

Try it if you like
British bitters

Great with
Tarte Tatin

Also try
La Choulette Bière
des Sans Culottes
7%, France

As it's been brewed since the 1920s, I think we can definitely call Jenlain Ambrée a classic.

A proudly independent brewery, Brassiere Duyck has remained in family hands, transforming over time but never changing its ethos of creating local beers first and foremost. The all-important ageing stage of around a month at a very cold temperature gives Jenlain its clean flavour, disguising the surprising level of booze!

With its aroma of crunchy autumn leaves, steamed orange pudding, warm spice and an almost savoury celery salt note, it is a delight for all the senses and one that I don't think gets enough attention.

WILD BEER CO WILD GOOSE CHASE

ABV
4.5%

Country of origin
UK

Try it if you like
Pinot Grigio

Great with
Elderflower fool

Also try
Lervig/Magic Rock
Farmhouse IPA
6%, Norway

Wild Beer Co is one of the most exciting breweries in the UK right now. Creating myriad farmhouse and modern ales that have so many twists they can make your head spin, they have truly committed to the farmhouse style by actually basing themselves on a farm in Somerset.

Wild Goose Chase is the beer that I've chosen to include in this section as it's a rare low ABV Saison, and one that I think could have easily been made by a farmer had the right ingredients been to hand.

It has a light gooseberry fruitiness, with just a hint of tartness, layered over the dryness of the wild yeast and the yoghurt astringency of lactobacillus from the local orchard yeast culture.

Perfect summer sipping, perhaps with a creamy dessert to stop it becoming cloying, it's a delicate work of brewing art.

LE BALADIN WAYAN

ABV
5.8%

Country of origin
Italy

Try it if you like
Gewürztraminer

Great with
Steak with green
peppercorn sauce

Also try
Birra del Borgo Duchessa
5.8%, Italy

The mad professor of Italian brewing (which is saying something!) Teo Musso, the founder of Baladin brewery, continues to pick up awards and turn out spectacular beers in equal measure.

Based in the Piedmont region, he is as entrenched in food as he is beer, and Wayan is just one of his beers that demonstrates that, with 17 different ingredients, including five grains (spelt, buckwheat, rye, barley and wheat) and nine spices, of which five are peppers – and none of which dominate.

On the nose you get pear and Earl Grey tea, with a hint of white pepper and coriander (cilantro), then on the palate it is lightly oily, with a hint of Cointreau and a bright, spicy finish.

IT'S ALWAYS CRUMPET SEASON

Makes 8–10

350 ml (11 fl oz/1⅓ cups)
  warm full-cream (whole) milk
1½ teaspoons golden caster
  (superfine) sugar
200 g (7 oz/1⅓ cups) strong
  white flour
150 g (5 oz/1 cup) plain
  (all-purpose) flour
4 teaspoons dried yeast
200 ml (7 fl oz/¾ cup) warm Saison
  such as Wayan
1½ teaspoons salt
1 teaspoon bicarbonate of soda
  (baking soda)
flavourless oil, for cooking
salted butter, to serve

Crumpets smothered in butter are one of the world's finest comfort foods, and I am genuinely chuffed to bits at the discovery that adding a little beer to the process makes them even more chewy and awesome. You will need metal cooking rings and a heavy-based frying pan for this – nothing else works as well.

Put the milk and sugar in a saucepan and start to warm over a very gentle heat.

Sift the flours and yeast into a bowl. Once the sugar has dissolved into the milk (which should be just hot enough that you can stand to put your pinkie into it, no more), pour it over the flour and mix briskly for about 5 minutes using a wooden spoon or stand mixer. Cover and leave to stand for 30 minutes–1 hour in a warm place.

Once the batter has risen and started to fall again, pop the beer and salt in a pan and start to gently warm. DO NOT LET IT BOIL. When the salt has dissolved and the beer is about the same temperature as the milk was, add half of it to the batter and then sprinkle the bicarbonate of soda on top. Mix quickly and keep adding more of the warm beer until you get a nice runny batter about the consistency of single (pouring) cream. Put back in the warm place for at least half an hour. It should be pretty bubbly before you start cooking.

Heat a heavy-based pan over a very low heat for at least 10 minutes so it is evenly hot. Grease the inside of the metal cooking rings. Place rings in pan to heat up.

Fill the rings with batter to about a third of the way up and leave, undisturbed, until the surface has set. After about 5 minutes you should have a gloriously bubbly surface. Carefully turn the rings over and ease a palette knife around the edges to release the crumpets. Cook on that side for a further 5–8 minutes or until just golden brown.

Repeat until you've used all the batter. Toast lightly, slather with butter and fill face!

SAISON JULEP

Serves 2
(in tumbler-style glasses)

300 ml (10 fl oz/1¼ cups) cold
    Saison (if it's flavoured or highly
    hopped, make sure it's citrus)
2 x 50 ml (2 fl oz/¼ cup) shots
    of decent bourbon (I use
    Four Roses)
10 mint leaves
2 teaspoons golden caster
    (superfine) sugar
crushed ice

A Saison really lends itself to a julep, making sure that
it's brisk and refreshing, and adds a little more body
than the usual soda water.

Divide the Saison between the glasses (I used Brew by
Numbers Motueka & Lime Saison). Pour a shot of bourbon
into each glass.

Muddle together the mint leaves and sugar and stir into
the Saison and bourbon until the sugar is dissolved.

Spoon in the crushed ice, stir softly and top with a fresh
mint leaf. Serve with some short straws.

CHAPTER NINE

WILD AND TAMED ONES

The most traditional examples of 'wild' beers are considered to be the Lambics of the Brussels area of Belgium. Protected under law, only beers produced in that area can be called Lambic - as a result you'll see beers from other areas of the world call themselves 'Lambic-style'.

But, as with everything, clever people find a way to recreate this styles all over the world, whether it's in Cambridge in the UK or San Diego in the USA - these traditional methods are being resurrected after being moth-balled for years.

All-in-all it is a tricky category to navigate because it heads into the world of the weird cousins of regular beers – you know the kind, the ones that you only invite to one party a year and even then they try to eat the candles on the birthday cake. So, with that rather worrying image in your mind, let's head off into the realms of wild yeast and bacterial fermentations.

Before you go, you'll see I talk about something called 'coolships' in this section; they are basically big, shallow copper swimming pools that the wort hangs out in to cool, which also allows the natural yeasts and bacteria in the air to settle on the beer and start what's known as the spontaneous fermentation process.

ORVAL

ABV
6.2%

Country of origin
Belgium

Try it if you like
Dry muscat or
farmhouse ciders

Great with
Roast pork belly or
mandarin cheesecake

Also try
Tilquin Oude Gueuze
à l'Ancienne
6.4%, Belgium

Like Madonna, Pelé and Picasso, Orval only needs one word to reduce its fans to misty-eyed, wobbly-kneed messes – and I don't mean from the alcoholic strength of it either.

Orval is one of those unicorn beers that make people say 'I don't like Brett beers but...' or 'I'm normally a wine or cider drinker but...' and even the most hardened, snobby sommelier has been known to say 'I don't like beer at all but...' It's just that unique.

A certified Trappist beer, it is brewed at the sensationally beautiful Orval Brewery in the Ardennes region of Belgium, and the key to this beer is how it changes as it ages, a cause of much debate amongst the seriously nerdy corner of the beer world.

If you are more of a dry, farmyard cider drinker, then the older versions are for you, but if you are looking to graduate from fresher, bitter beers like IPAs, then younger, orangey hop-forward versions are a good place to start. You can find the bottling date on the label to help you out with your choice.

BRASSERIE DE LA SENNE BRUXELLENSIS

ABV
6.5%

Country of origin
Belgium

Try it if you like
Fruity, leathery whiskies

Great with
Confit duck leg

Also try
Boon Oude Geuze
Mariage Parfait
8%, Belgium

Whisper the name 'Yvan de Baets' in beer circles and you'll get a knowing nod. Along with his incredibly friendly and hospitable business partner Bernard Leboucq, he started the brewery by cuckoo brewing, but they now have their own home in the suburbs of Brussels (where they have a fermentation room that looks like a church, stained glass windows and all).

Bruxellensis is an unsurprising move for the pair, with Brussels being the only place where you can make a beer and call it 'Lambic', due to the unique yeast and bacteria in the air. However, the inoculation of this beer happens in the bottle instead of in big coolships.

The flavours are intense and too many to list here in full, but expect full-on red berry fruit on the nose, with a hint of pear, and a dry as a bone leathery finish, with a vibrant earthy pepperiness.

ELGOOD'S COOLSHIP DARK

ABV
6%

Country of origin
UK

Try it if you like
Barolo

Great with
Venison stew

Also try
Rodenbach Grand Cru
6%, Belgium

In a quiet, unassuming area of Cambridge sits Elgood's Brewery, which was until a few years ago a sleepy, traditional brewery that quite often won national awards for its dark, mild Black Dog.

Then, when Nigel Elgood retired, he handed the running of the brewery over to his three daughters and, pow, they turned the brewery's image on its head, resurrecting the long-defunct coolship to make new beers in the very old Belgian Lambic-style.

After a bit of research they realised that they were in prime territory to make proper 'wild' beers, as fruit trees abound all around Cambridge, so they set about cladding the walls of the coolship room with some old oak planks that had been seasoning for over a decade in the grounds, and thus the beers were born. There are three versions available: the Blonde, a blended gueuze-style beer, is fairly regular, while the Dark and the Fruit are more sporadic.

The flavours are rich, dark fruits, treacle toffee, leather, oak and the merest hint of marzipan. It's an exquisite beer that even the Belgians would be proud of – it should be supped slowly and savoured.

LOST ABBEY DUCK DUCK GOOZE

ABV
7%

Country of origin
USA

Try it if you like
Fino sherry

Great with
Oysters

Also try
Grutte Pier Tripel
Uit De Ton
8%, Netherlands

Although I don't want to put lots of rare or difficult to find beers in here, it's hard to avoid in this section as these beers take so long to make and the yield is so low.

Much as it would be tempting to make a joke about only choosing this one for its name (it is, after all, a most excellent pun), I haven't – it's all about the beer.

In fact, if you get into your sours then just keep an eye out for Lost Abbey beers full stop. Brewmaster Tomme Arthur sure knows what he's doing.

Duck Duck Gooze is a homage to the gueuze style of beer from Belgium and, just like those beers, it is a blend of old and young beers from different barrels.

The initial impact is like drinking white balsamic from a leather gourd (I mean that in a good way, odd as it sounds), but it's soon joined by some wood complexity and flirty notes of sea buckthorn. It's a palate awakener extraordinaire.

ORIGINAL RITTERGUTS GOSE

ABV
4.7%

Country of origin
Germany

Try it if you like
Sherbet

Great with
Fried chicken

Also try
10 Barrel Brewing
Cucumber Crush
5%, USA

There's a lot to be said for the theory that the beer revolution has been driven by the curiosity of home brewers and their desire to dig deep and often, if a lot of my friends are anything to go by, out nerd each other!

In this case, it was a German home brewer, Tilo Janichen ,who decided that it was vital he resurrect the style of his local area, Leipzig, and set about finding breweries to work with to do so.

Most of the Goses you will find these days have fruit added to them, but this is brewed in the traditional style, with coriander seeds and sea salt, and is soured naturally with lactobacillus, making it very tart, refreshing, light, savoury and a little spicy.

DUCK WITH FLANDERS CHERRY SAUCE, POTATOES AND GREENS

Serves 2

1 tablespoon olive, grapeseed or
    groundnut (peanut) oil
½ onion, finely chopped
3 sprigs of thyme
2 garlic cloves, smashed to a
    paste with some salt
1 tin of cherries
2 confit de canard (precooked
    duck legs preserved in fat),
    either tin or vacuum packed
fine sea salt and freshly ground
    black pepper
350 g (12 oz) new potatoes,
    boiled, chilled and sliced into
    2 cm (¾ inch) thick discs
2 knobs of unsalted butter
bitter greens, like Savoy
    cabbage, cavolo nero or kale
1 bottle of Flanders-style beer,
    like Rodenbach Grand Cru

This is a ridiculously simple but slightly flashy dish, perfect for laid-back dinner parties.

Preheat your oven to 160°C (320°F/Gas 3).

Heat a saucepan on a medium heat and add the oil. Sweat half the chopped onions with a sprig of thyme until the onions are translucent. Add half the smashed garlic and sauté for 30 seconds. Stir in the tinned cherries with the juice and continue cooking for 5 minutes. Set aside and allow to cool a little.

Heat a large frying pan (skillet) on a medium heat and remove the duck legs from their tin or vacuum packed bag. Place them, and all the fat in the packaging, into the pan. Gently brown the duck legs on both sides, season, then gently remove them from the pan and place on a baking tray in the oven, to finish cooking gently. Reserve the fat – it's where the flavour is.

Remove the thyme sprig from the cherry mixture. Blitz the mixture in a blender (or use a stick blender), then set over a low heat to reduce to a thick, gloopy sauce. Remove from the heat and set aside.

Reheat the duck fat, and add the potatoes. Gently brown on one side then flip them over and add the remaining onions, garlic and thyme leaves. Add half the butter and shake the pan to coat the potates in all the flavours.

Take the duck legs out of the oven and allow to rest a little, before plating. Steam the greens then place on the plates with the duck legs. Dish out the slices of cooked, buttery, thyme potatoes.

Return the cherry sauce to the heat, and add the remaining butter with 100 ml (3½ fl oz) of Rodenbach (you can also use a cherry beer if you want). Gently warm through then pour over the duck, greens and potoes.

Serve immdietely with a glass of the remaining Rodenbach and enjoy!

NINKASI'S KISS

Serves 2

30 ml (1 fl oz/⅛ cup)
    Noilly Prat vermouth
50 ml (2 fl oz/¼ cup)
    elderflower liqueur
    (I use Chase)
1 egg white
2 teaspoons simple syrup*
½ teaspoon yuzu juice
2 ice cubes
200 ml (7 fl oz) Orval
    (or Wild Beer Co. Ninkasi)
a pinch of sumac, to finish

Named for the Sumerian Goddess of Beer (and because I used Wild Beer Co's Ninkasi in the original recipe which I also recommend) this cocktail can add a little kiss of sophistication to your beer drinking repertoire.

Put the vermouth, elderflower liqueur, egg white, syrup and yuzu juice in a shaker with the ice cubes, shake for 20 seconds and strain into 2 flutes.

Top carefully with ale as it will fizz up (but it does look good with a bit of a head of both beer foam and egg emulsion on it). Sprinkle with sumac and serve.

* Simple syrup is equal parts sugar and water warmed gently until the sugar dissolves and then cooled again.

CHAPTER TEN

THE
DARK
SIDE

Dark beers get a really bad rep, and they really don't deserve it. People seem to think they are heavier, more calorific or all taste the same - basically people equate dark beer with that ubiquitous Irish brand that you see all over the world and have never tried something like, say, Moorhouse's Black Cat Mild, which is as light and refreshing as they come.

Now I'm not saying that Guinness is particularly bad, I don't think it's particularly good, but its serving method using nitrogen, which has very tiny bubbles and makes the beer seem thicker and more viscous, has a lot to do with this misconception that all beers are the same, they aren't!

So, I'd like you to think about these beers differently and don't just drink with your eyes. Do you like chocolate, coffee, dark fruits and fruit cakes? If you like one or all of those things, then I can almost guarantee that you will like some or all of the beers in this section.

Oh, and before you go, I just want to bust a myth that just won't go away... there isn't any iron in dark beers (or any beers for that matter) but all beer does contain niacin, which is a vital precursor for the uptake of iron in the blood. Another good pub quiz fact!

LA SIRÈNE PRALINE

ABV
6%

Country of origin
Australia

Try it if you like
Praline chocolates

Great with
Raspberry ripple
ice cream

Also try
Cigar City
Marshal Zhukov's
Penultimate Push
11.5%, USA

In the UK, there is a woodstain called Ronseal whose slogan is 'Does exactly what it says on the tin'. This is what we would colloquially call a Ronseal beer.

La Sirène is a brewery that fascinated me long before I'd got my hands on any of its brews. It seemed to tick all the boxes – elegant branding, a great attitude on social media and love from a lot of people that I respect – so I'm so pleased it didn't disappoint when I finally got to try some at the Pacific Beer Expo in Wellington, New Zealand.

Although they specialise in farmhouse ales, it's this one that really took my breath away, which is saying something considering how good their Saisons are. Using a Belgian stout as its base (a dark beer using a fruity Belgian yeast), it's made with what are basically the ingredients for Nutella®, and that's exactly what it tastes like – a boozy version of everyone's favourite chocolate spread.

The sweet, unctuous body comes from the use of both lactose and hazelnuts, meaning this beer punches well above its 6% ABV weight.

ODELL CUTTHROAT PORTER

ABV
5%

Country of origin
USA

Try it if you like
Stouts

Great with
Raclette cheese

Also try
Neptune Brewery Abyss
5%, UK

Doug Odell is one of my heroes in the brewing world and I've never met anyone in the industry with a bad word to say about him.

In a portfolio of beers with exceptional balance and elegance, this is still, despite me changing my mind a hundred times, my favourite beer from his brewery.

Named after the Coloradan state fish (yes, there really is such a thing!), it's like someone made a fruit cake, added some cocoa and then smothered it in blackcurrant jam – a description I've used before, but one I can't seem to better when describing this beer.

Designed to sit somewhere in between a porter and a stout, it offers a lot of the richness of the latter and the drinkability of the former, and when I finally get the chance to grab a fly rod and go fishing for these notoriously fearsome fighting fish, I will make sure I have a bottle in my bag to celebrate or, more likely, commiserate at the end of the day.

BODEBROWN BLACK RYE IPA

ABV
7%

Country of origin
Brazil

Try it if you like
80% cocoa chocolate

Great with
Panna cotta

Also try
The Kernel Export
India Porter
6%, UK

Bodebrown is Brazil's answer to the lunatic fringe of brewing. Headed up by the brilliantly bonkers Sammo Cabral, this brewery always brings the fun.

Often using lots of interesting Brazilian woods for its beers, like the root beer-esque emberana, this is the one that I've chosen due to its wider availability and its understanding of balance in what is often a very unbalanced interpretation of a slightly silly style. After all, the notion of a black India pale ale is the epitome of an oxymoron.

However, if you think of this as more of a well-hopped porter-style beer it makes much more sense, with all the big grapefruit and tropical fruit aroma of a US-style IPA and the spicy, chocolate body and drinkability of a UK porter, it is a great beer to experiment with.

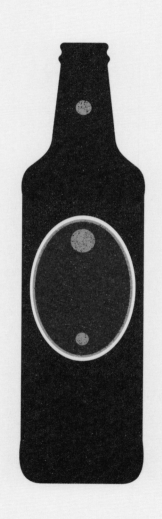

FULLER'S IMPERIAL STOUT

ABV
10.7%

Country of origin
UK

Try it if you like
Chocolate-covered
Turkish delight

Great with
Fondue

Also try
Amundsen Bryggeri
Dessert in a Can
Chocolate Marshmallow
10%, Norway

I'm being rather self-indulgent by including a second collaboration beer of mine in here, but I am so very proud to have brewed with my local brewery Fuller's that I can't resist (it's also the second beer from Fuller's, but I am a firm believer in cheering for your home team, so for that I won't apologise!)

This all came about due to my childhood fascination with the Fry's Turkish Delight chocolate bar. It tempted me with its exotic pink hue and repulsed me with its concentrated jelly and rose petal interior, so when I got old enough (I'm not claiming grown up by any means), I decided to brew a boozy version.

The beer ticks every box I wanted it to – with its rosy, geraniol and chocolate nose, its thick, luscious body with a hint of espresso, and its lingering, lightly roasted bitter finish with just a hint of that signature Fuller's orange blossom yeast. I can't urge you strongly enough to buy a few bottles and lay them down to age. And just in case you think I'm promoting any of my collab beers for personal gain, I want to reassure you I don't earn a penny from any of them.

BAX BIER
KOUD VUUR

ABV
6.3%

Country of origin
Netherlands

Try it if you like
Smoky whiskies

Great with
Braised beef ribs

Also try
Durham Brewery
Temptation
10%, UK

Baxbier is from one of my favourite places in the world, Groningen. It may seem like an odd place to love, but it holds one of the best independent beer festivals with the warmest welcomes ever.

Baxbier is a success story I have kept an eye on from the start. They've gone from being stocked just locally to being sought after all over the country, and word is getting out about them internationally too.

The Koud Vuur is, for me, their most accomplished beer – delicately smoky, full of blackcurrant and bramble fruits and with a thirst-slaking dry finish.

These young men have a serious future ahead of them, which is just as well as they've built a pretty big brewery on the outskirts of the town. However, I have faith that they will outgrow even that in the next five years.

GOOD GEORGE ROCKY ROAD

ABV
5%

Country of origin
New Zealand

Try it if you like
Rocky road ice cream

Great with
Child-like glee

Also try
Brouwerij Martinus
Smoked Porter
9%, Netherlands

There's nothing like a beer that makes you giggle, even though it's the first one of the day. That's what this beer did for me when I first tried it as I arrived on the shores of Lake Taupo in New Zealand and settled into the local beer café.

Another 'Ronseal' beer, meaning it does quite literally what it says on the tin – and in a tin it does indeed come. Modern cans are great for beer, as they prevent damage from light and oxygen and could be more environmentally friendly than bottles.

Rocky Road is the result of Good George joining forces with local chocolatiers Donovan's to make some seriously good time beers. The flavours are individually clear as a bell – raspberry, chocolate and vanilla – but they also harmonise to give you that feeling of drinking a bowl of booze-spiked rocky road. I applaud any brewery that can achieve that technical feat so flawlessly and yet still talk about it with childish glee.

FYNE ALES VITAL SPARK

ABV
4.4%

Country of origin
UK

Try it if you like
Dark lager

Great with
Mature Cheddar cheese

Also try
Birrificio del Ducato Verdi
8.2%, Italy

Mild beer is a matter of much historic debate, but I will always bow to the beer historian Martyn Cornell on the definition. He says they were thus-named as they were 'fresh' beers, as opposed to having some age on them, and also, as a result, had less hop character. However, they were by no means unhopped or low alcohol as a lot of people seem to want to rewrite them as.

Fyne Ales' version in Vital Spark certainly brings the word 'fresh' to mind when you drink it, because it is just that. Lean of body and hopped with the tropical Amarillo and grapefruity Cascade, both being applied sparingly. I almost wish that the brewery, a genuine gem hiding up in Argyll in Scotland, was somewhere more metropolitan so they could get all the plaudits that I think they deserve, but then perhaps they wouldn't have the quiet, contemplative approach to great beer making if they were. Either way, grab anything of theirs you see. You won't regret it.

MILD CUSTARD

Makes 8–10

200 ml (7 fl oz/¾ cup)
    double (thick) cream
700 ml (23 fl oz/2¾ cups)
    full-cream (whole) milk
3 tablespoons cornflour
    (cornstarch)
8 tablespoons mild beer
4 large egg yolks
185 g (6½ oz/1 cup) caster
    (superfine) sugar
1 tablespoon maple syrup
1 teaspoon vanilla bean paste

Sometimes a small change is what makes all the difference, and that's exactly what this is here - you don't have to add a lot of the beer for it to add a really rich, moreish edge to the custard. It's subtle but it's really tasty!

Place the cream and milk in a pan and gently bring to just below boiling point.

Meanwhile, in a large bowl, combine the cornflour with the beer, and whisk with the egg yolks, sugar, maple syrup and vanilla bean paste.

Slowly add the warm cream/milk mixture to the egg/sugar mix and whisk briskly.

Add back to the saucepan and warm slowly, stirring constantly with a wooden spoon, until the custard sticks well to the back of it. Set aside with a piece of baking paper on top to stop a skin forming or pour straight into a jug and serve over apple crumble or pie.

PEAT NUT MONSTER

Serves 2
(in tumbler-style glasses)

2 ice cubes
100 ml (3½ fl oz/scant ½ cup)
   peated whisky
1 handful of peanut butter
   M&Ms® or Reese's Pieces®
500 ml (17 fl oz/2 cups) Imperial
   Stout, at room temperature

My other half thinks I'm crackers for liking this cocktail. In fact, he looked at me with such utter horror when I made it that I genuinely considered not putting it in here, but I really liked it so, nerrrrrr.

Let me know whether you think I'm an absolute monster or a genius for this via social media – but only with a picture of the cocktail. If you haven't tried it, you don't get a say!

Blitz the ingredients in a blender until totally combined. Pass through a fine sieve into a shaker, top up with beer and stir gently. Pour into 2 tumblers to serve.

CHAPTER ELEVEN

BIG BEERS

A bit of an all-encompassing header I know, but when you want to sit down in your wing-back leather chair wearing your smoking jacket (everyone has these right?) or perhaps just with a cheese board, this is the section you need.

Some of these beers can easily take the place of bold reds or fortified wines, but they can also compete with complex Rieslings and sherries, perhaps because they've been aged in their barrels and sometimes just because they've been well oxidised, giving them the same characteristics. Either way, their complexity and strength should complement each other. Alcoholic strength is just a contributory factor to their fabulousness. It is also why you won't see a cocktail recipe in this section, as it would seem a little short-sighted to attempt to kill off my readership!

Some questions I get asked regularly are 'What glass should I drink this out of?' and 'What temperature is best for this beer?' And I normally answer, 'However the hell you like it.' But, when it comes to beers like this, I would like to offer some advice. Drink this beer lightly chilled, meaning take it out of the fridge at least half an hour before you want to drink it, and pour it with a decent head (if you can get one) into a brandy balloon or just a big-bowled wine glass. Perfection.

GOOSE ISLAND BOURBON COUNTY STOUT

ABV
Varies

Country of origin
USA

Try it if you like
Bourbon

Great with
Honking rind-washed cheese

Also try
New Holland Dragon's Milk 11%, USA

What do you do when you're a beer- and bourbon-loving brewmaster at a Chicago brewery and you want to celebrate its thousandth brew? Well, if you're Greg Hall, you bring the two together to create an industry icon.

The idea for BCS was born from a chance meeting between Hall and the master distiller of Jim Beam. Hall talked the man into giving him some barrels for a beer and the die was cast.

Goose Island nearly broke the kit loading all the malt to make the Russian Imperial Stout that would become the basis of the beer. But when they poured it into barrels and inhaled that distinctive vanilla and coconut, they knew they were on to a winner.

As you enjoy BCS, you can breathe in the heady aroma of pure dark chocolate, sumptuous vanilla, perky espresso and, of course, bourbon. On the palate it's like a grown-up chocolate milkshake that greets you with a big ol' warming tummy hug.

ROCHEFORT 10

ABV
11.3%

Country of origin
Belgium

Try it if you like
Pedro Ximénez

Great with
Prune cake (Far Breton)

Also try
St Bernardus ABT 12
10%, Belgium

I'm not known for entering a room quietly, but even I was amazed at the stir I caused when I visited Rochefort. The day I went with a couple of other beer writers there was a foot of snow on the ground and a fairly unpleasant, sleeting storm outside as we walked across the enormous grounds of the abbey to the brew house. It was only when I felt warm enough to take my hood down and scarf off my face that the 'mistake' was discovered.

According to the Prior who was conducting our tour, I was the first woman to be allowed, albeit accidentally, into all areas of the brewery. I have no idea whether it's true or not, but I'm not about to start calling senior monks fibbers!

Rochefort 10 is, quite simply, a god-given nectar. Prunes, raisins, currants, dried cranberries, apricots, cinnamon, nutmeg, orange peel, brandy, Pedro Ximénez sherry and so much more abound in this beer. A warning though – it's dangerously strong, so do be careful if you're going in for a second, or at least make sure you're sitting down!

J.W. LEES HARVEST ALE

ABV
11.5%

Country of origin
UK

Try it if you like
Tawny Port

Great with
Stilton cheese

Also try
Fuller's Vintage,
8.5%, UK

I love it when a beer has a great story behind it, especially one with a bit pride, and this one has exactly that. During a brewer's dinner in the mid-80s everyone was chuntering about the rampant takeover of lager (or 'eurofizz' as it was rather childishly nick named) and so the then head brewer of Lees decided that he would showcase the very finest of the UK's barley and hop crop and make a harvest ale.

A nod to the UK tradition of churches and schools getting together to celebrate and give thanks for the gathering of crops, it uses East Kent Goldings and British barley and that's it. Its heady 11.5% alcohol content means when it is fresh it is redolent with fruit cake, maple syrup and orange rind but, as it ages, it becomes more oxidised and like fortified wine.

In fact, some of the older bottles I have opened have so many madeira, port and sherry characteristics that it is almost impossible to think of them in any other terms than beers for a special occasion - which can just be a Tuesday around here!

DE MOLEN
WEER & WIND

ABV
12.4%

Country of origin
Netherlands

Try it if you like
Bourbon

Great with
Braised beef cheeks

Also try
Brasserie Dieu du
Ciel Péché Mortel
9.5%, Canada

If you fancy a trip to an epic beer festival in September, then you should head to the Borefts festival that De Molen organise. It's quite the party, with hundreds of beers from some of the world's most sought-after breweries. But do remember, it's a marathon, not a sprint!

Anyway, Weer & Wind is a close cousin to my personal favourite Bommen & Granaten, but this is such a close second and since I'm slightly in the minority when choosing between the two, I thought I'd bow to majority rule for a change!

Although there is a dominant note from the bourbon barrel it's aged in, underneath it all there is a rich, toffee malt base and chocolate and lime notes from the Premiant hops, which offset the beer just enough to make it not too cloying.

RENAISSANCE BREWING TRIBUTE

ABV
10.8%

Country of origin
New Zealand

Try it if you like
Speyside whisky

Great with
A comfortable chair

Also try
Harviestoun Ola Dubh
8%, UK

The tiny Reniassance Brewing headquarters are tucked away next to a very eccentric pub in Nelson, at the heart of New Zealand's wine country.

Run by a Brit and an American, the brewery has that glorious Heath Robinson aspect to it that I deeply admire in this industry, where people have found a way to ply their passion for beer over and above what their ability to invest in state-of-the-art equipment would imply.

Made to an Elizabethan recipe, Tribute undergoes a prolonged cellaring time, which allows the yeast to do a number of things, but most importantly it's not big, hot and boozy. Instead, even at 10.8%, it's elegant and refined, with hints of Chateau d'Yquem on the nose, a balanced honey, Marmite and golden syrup to it, and a warming, almost jasmine tea-like finish.

Sure, this would be great with lots of different foods – it would be fantastic with sweetbreads or, if you are comfortable with it, foie gras – but the best way I've found to enjoy this beer is sipped slowly by itself in a mellow moment of contemplation, with a good book and listening to Miles Davis.

MEGA MALT LOAF

Makes 1 loaf
(23 cm × 13 cm/5 in × 9 in)

75 ml (2½ fl oz/⅓ cup) strong,
    cold black tea
75 ml (2½ fl oz/⅓ cup) Rochefort 10
unsalted butter, to grease
100 g (3½ fl oz/⅓ cup) raisins
100 g (3½ oz/⅔ cup) chopped,
    pitted dates
100 g (3½ oz/½ cup) prunes
175 g (6 oz) malt extract
(liquid form)
85 g (3 oz/scant ½ cup) dark
    muscovado sugar (do not
    substitute)
2 large eggs, beaten
100 g (3½ oz/⅖ cup) wholemeal
    (whole-wheat) flour
150 g (5 oz/1 cup) plain
    (all-purpose) flour
1 teaspoon bicarbonate of soda
    (baking soda)
2 teaspoons baking powder
SALTED BUTTER (this is in caps
    deliberately, as it is my firm
    belief that you can't properly
    enjoy malt loaf without salted
    butter), to serve

For the malt glaze
4 tablespoons malt extract
    liquid form)
1 tablespoon Rochefort 10

I love malt loaf; its been a fixture in my life for as long as I can remember. It was my mum who introduced the edict of 'always toasted, always dripping in butter' and you don't argue with mums, it's the law!

In a saucepan, gently heat the tea and beer until bubbles just start to break the surface. Remove from the heat, add the dried fruit and leave to stand for 15 minutes.

Preheat the oven to 150°C (300°F/Gas 2). Using unsalted butter, grease and line a loaf tin with baking paper.

Pour the warm tea, beer and dried fruit mixture into a mixing bowl with the malt extract and sugar, stirring well until the sugar is fully dissolved. Keep stirring and add the eggs.

In a separate bowl, mix together the flours, bicarbonate of soda and baking powder. Add the liquid ingredients to the flour, stirring vigorously, and leave to stand for 15 minutes.

Bake for 50 minutes until well risen and firm to the touch.

While the cake is still hot, warm the malt extract and beer together in a saucepan over a medium heat for about 10 minutes, swirling from time to time and making sure it does not boil. Poke holes into the loaf with a sharp knife. Paint the cake liberally with the malt and beer mix, allowing it to seep into the holes. Wrap in baking paper and cling film.

This loaf gets better after three or four days. You should ALWAYS eat it with lashings of salty butter and, if you can manage to wait, warming it lightly in the toaster or under the grill (broiler) only makes it better.

CHAPTER TWELVE

NO, LOW AND G-FREE BEERS

Believe it or not, there are times when I really, really wish there was a decent low- or no-alcohol beer on hand. It might be one of the rare occasions when I'm driving and I actually just don't want to drink sweet, fizzy nonsense all evening, but options are all too often few and far between.

And, while not being gluten intolerant or suffering from coeliac disease myself, my heart goes out to those who can't have gluten and may feel they are deprived of beer.

So, while I think that genuine high-quality beers of this ilk are still too difficult to get your hands on, there are a number spread over the world that I think are well worth drinking for aesthetic reasons as much as any other.

It's worth noting that, in most places in the world, anything below 0.5% is considered non-alcoholic and is physically impossible to get drunk on, so please don't think when it says 0.5% that I'm being dim (although anyone who knows my legendary lack of numeric capabilities could easily believe otherwise!).

BIG DROP CHOCOLATE MILK STOUT

ABV
0.5%

Country of origin
UK

Try it if you like
Cold brew coffee with
a chocolate muffin

Great with
Spicy beef curry

Also try
Bernard Free Sour Cherry
0.5%, Czech Republic

The idea for Big Drop Brewing Co. came from founder Rob Fink, who decided he needed to give up the booze after a bender to end all benders (a promise I think we've probably all made to ourselves at some point in time!) and his search for a decent no or low alcohol substitute proved fairly fruitless.

So, after teaming up with a school friend, designer James Kindred, they then recruited Johnny Clayton (formerly of Wild Beer Co.) to create a low alcohol beer with depth and flavour and Big Drop. was properly born.

A game-changer for the low/no alcohol market and the only thing that doesn't register as a full-blooded beer is a slight lack of body which is often provided by alcohol but that's it, otherwise it tastes exactly like a milk stout, full of vanilla, powdered milk and coffee flavours.

GREEN'S DRY-HOPPED LAGER

ABV
4%

Country of origin
Belgium

Try it if you like
Pale ales

Great with
Friends or a hot day

Also try
Leeds Brewery
Original 0PA
0%, UK

Full of vibrant, zesty hop character and zippy, clean refreshment, Green's has come a very long way from its origins when, frankly, the beers were pretty average... although I'm sure to a beer-deprived coeliac they were a godsend!

Although a UK-owned company, the beers are brewed in Belgium at the only brewery that, back in the early 2000s, finally agreed to help Derek Green in his 20-year quest to make gluten-free beers after he was diagnosed and forced to cut out barley and wheat.

A chance meeting with a brewing professor whose daughter couldn't eat gluten either, and the dream was born. There's now a whole range, all of which I could recommend, but the dry-hopped lager is my favourite.

GLUTENBERG AMERICAN PALE ALE

ABV
5.5%

Country of origin
Canada

Try it if you like
Fruit cocktail

Great with
Montreal smoked meat
or pastrami

Also try
Westerham Brewery Co.
Scotney Pale Ale
4%, UK

Glutenberg was the first brewery's beers that I tried and honestly thought, 'I like that', rather than 'that's OK for a gluten-free beer', and their flagship pale ale still continues to delight.

It has all the fresh, vibrant grapefruit and lime with a hint of pine that you'd expect from an American-style pale ale. This beer is perfect to keep in the fridge and drink while you contemplate dinner after a long, hard day at work. I am also a huge fan of the IPA these guys produce – it's very polished.

MIKKELLER DRINK'IN THE SUN

ABV
0.3%

Country of origin
Denmark

Try it if you like
Cloudy lemonade

Great with
Grilled white fish

Also try
Arcobräu Urfass
Alcohol-Free 0.5%,
Germany

It's no big surprise that the daddy of cuckoo brewing, Mikkel Borg Bjergsø, was one of the first 'craft' brewers to come up with a low-alcohol beer full of flavour. Since he turns out ideas as fast as most of us breathe, it surprises me it took him as long as it did.

An American-style wheat beer, this is straightforward lemony, peachy refreshment at its finest and shouldn't be pressed into service with anything more complicated than a piece of grilled fish or chicken with a green salad – but then sometimes simple is all you need.

ERDINGER ALKOHOLFREI

ABV
0.5%

Country of origin
Germany

Try it if you like
Running marathons

Great with
A sweat on

Also try
Fentimans Lemon Shandy
0.5%, UK

I love that this is being marketed as an isotonic drink for people post-exercise. In fairness to Erdinger, there have been studies done that show that a low-alcohol beer consumed directly after exercising is very good for you and will help you recover quicker than anything except a sports drink. This alcohol-free version has the benefit of being lower in calories than most sports drinks, too.

It is a bit more muted than most German-style wheat beers, but that's not necessarily a bad thing if you find the banana and clove notes of the yeast overwhelming. Besides, ice-cold after a workout, any beer tastes good, and this has an extra healthier smug factor thrown in.

NEW BELGIUM GLÜTINY GOLDEN ALE

ABV
5.2%

Country of origin
USA

Try it if you like
Lager

Great with
Tacos

Also try
Wold Top Against the Grain
4.5%, UK

New Belgium is one of those places you dream of working; an employee-owned business with serious ethical, environmental and social credentials.

Just so you know, you'll see on the website or the bottle, some very carefully-worded blather about the fact that it's 'crafted to be reduced gluten' - which could easily be mistaken for marketing horse manure.

However, don't blame New Belgium or any other US brewery, as the FDA, unlike most other places in the world, refuses to allow any business to use gluten-free, one assume because there are thousands of lawyers sitting around sharpening lawsuits about it.

Anyway, bureaucratic nonsense aside, this (and its sibling the Glutiny pale ale) is an intensely refreshing beer with gentle buttering and aroma lovely leathery Goldings hops and a bit more punch from the Cascade and Nugget.

GLUTEN-FREE BEER-BRINED CHICKEN KIEV

Serves 2

For the beer brine
500 ml (17 fl oz) bottle
    of any g-free golden ale
generous pinch of salt
1 garlic clove, smashed
1 strip of lemon zest
½ teaspoon black peppercorns,
    toasted and crushed
1 bay leaf

For the kievs
2 large chicken breasts
1 bulb garlic, roasted *
coarse sea salt
50 g (2 oz/¼ cup) butter
    at room temperature
2 tablespoons finely chopped
    fresh parsley
1 tablespoon finely chopped
    fresh tarragon
50 g (2 oz/⅓ cup)
    gluten-free flour
1 egg, whisked with a little milk
100 g (3½ oz/½ cup) polenta
    (cornmeal)
vegetable spray oil

Chicken kiev needs no introduction so what I'll say here is that I always make extra of the roast garlic butter. Officially called a compound butter, you can use it on everything from finishing a steak or pasta dish to slathering on top of a roast chicken.

Warm the beer and 500 ml (17 fl oz/2 cups) water gently together in a pan, then add the salt and the remaining beer brine ingredients and stir until the salt dissolves. Leave to cool. When it's cool, add the chicken breasts, cover and leave to brine for at least 6 hours in the fridge.

Smash the roasted garlic cloves into a paste with a little coarse sea salt, then smash that into the butter along with the herbs, roll into a cylinder and put in the fridge to firm up. This can be done long in advance.

When you're ready to assemble the kievs, take the chicken from the brine and pat it dry. Cut a slit in each breast and pop half the cylinder of butter inside each one, squeezing the flesh closed behind it.

Dust each chicken breast in the flour, roll it in the egg mix and then finally in the polenta.

Place in the fridge for an hour. After 45 minutes, preheat the oven with a baking tray to 180°C (350°F/Gas 4).

When the hour is up, take the chicken out, spray it all over with oil, pop on the baking tray and cook for 20–25 minutes. Serve with chips and corn on the cob.

* It's incredibly simple to roast a whole garlic bulb. Simply slice the head off the garlic, drizzle with a little oil, and wrap in foil. Roast in the oven at 180°C (350°F/Gas 4) for 20–25 minutes, until soft and sweet.

BIG FLOAT

Serves 2

1 bottle of Big Drop Chocolate
    Milk Stout
300 ml (10 fl oz/1¼ cups) fiery
    ginger beer
chocolate ice cream
sprinkles, to top

Embrace your inner child and succumb to a fiery ginger
and chocolate beer float... go on, you know you want to!

Divide the Big Drop between two pint glasses, top up with
ginger beer, add a scoop of chocolate ice cream and apply
sprinkles with the abandon of a hyperactive three-year-old.

Award-winning beer and food writer Melissa Cole's passion in life is getting people to learn as little as much as they like about what she considers the finest social lubricant known to man.

Respected the world over for her fine palate, she is invited to judge at competitions in places as far flung as New Zealand, the US and Brazil, as well as closer to home across Europe, aware of the impact this can have the future of breweries she has also spent years educating herself on the brewing process, often getting her hands dirty and making beers with some of the best breweries across the globe.

Melissa's other passion is food and she is recognised as probably the UK's leading expert in pairing and cooking with beer, having spent years dedicated to figuring out which beers work in which dishes and why - which she regularly calls 'making a whole series of disgusting mistakes, so you don't have to'.

This is Melissa's second book and keeps true to her passion for simple beer communication that neither baffles nor patronises the audience, she just wants people to enjoy beer as much as she does!

THANK YOU

Firstly, thank you to the team at Hardie Grant – you are all an utter dream to work with, I'm blessed to have found you.

A huge thanks to Stuart Hardie for his amazing design skills and illustrations.

Ben, as always, you are my rock, I love you.

My family, you always put up with me and support my mad schemes and crazy career – I love you all more than words can express. Special shout out to my in-laws Pam and Stan, this is all your fault you know! And, of course, my 'mini me' Kate, keep being fabulous.

My drinking partners in crime: Richard Dinwoodie, Mike Hill, Jamie Kenyon, Dan Fox, Andy Martin and Alberta Bussett – thank you all for being there and the same goes for those friends who I don't see very often, Miya Canty, Christine Warren-White, Caroline Mair and Gillian Robson, we don't see each other nearly enough but I know you're always there and I adore you. And, of course, Sharona Selby – no one gives hilariously weird hugs like you.

Professionally (and personally because it's that kind of industry) I owe a gajillion people thank yous but there are a few folk I really do want to acknowledge: the first is John Keeling, I was immensely humbled when you agreed to write the foreword to this and thank you for your support over the years, and of course the sarcasm, you do it so well.

Roger Ryman, Derek Prentice, Kelly Ryan, Stuart Howe, John Driebergen, Henry Chevallier-Guild, Georgina Young, Chris Swersey, Angus McKean and Claire Morgan, Hannah Sharman-Cox, Joanna Dring, Doug Odell, Simon Pipola, Maik and Arianna Van Heerd, the whole Falling Rock family, Mark Tranter and Luc de Raedemaeker.

Colleagues like Roger Protz, Adrian Tierney-Jones, Tim Hampson, Sophie Atherton, Matt Curtis and Pete Brown you all inspire me and keep me on my toes. And thanks to everyone at the Rake for taking in my post and feeding me lots of excellent beer.

To all the chefs and food writers I have bounced ideas off over the years, thank you so much (especially you Alyn Williams) and for those of you who have done me the honour of stealing my recipes and pretending to pass them off as your own (that'll be you Si Toft).

To all the folks on Twitter, Facebook and Instagram who support me and make me laugh when I'm going ballistic and put up with my extremely creative language at times, thank you, you're all fabulous.

And finally, to the women of the beer, pub and restaurant industry – especially the Crafty Beer Girls – you brilliant, smart, feisty women keep me going when the fight against sexism feels like it's just too much – you inspire me every single day to keep going with your strength and convictions.

BEER INDEX

2 Cabeças/Cevejaria Dadiva
Pink Lemonade 105
7 Peaks La Dent Jaune 24
8 Wired Feijoa 109
10 Barrel Brewing
Cucumber Crush 131
21st Amendment Hell
or High Watermelon 104

A

Aecht Schlenkerla
Rauchbier Märzen 77
Alesmith Nut Brown Ale 80
Amundsen Bryggeri Dessert
In A Can Chocolate
Marshmallow 141
Anchor Steam Beer 84
Anspach & Hobday
Smoked Brown 77
Arcobräu Urfass
Alcohol-Free 165
Augustiner-Bräu Dunkel 31

Australia

Feral Brewing Co. White 48
La Sirène Praline 137
Little Creatures Rogers' 76
Moo Brew Hefeweizen 49
Pirate Life IPA 61
Stone & Wood Pacific Ale 65
Two Birds Bantam IPA 68

B

Bagby Beer Three
Beagles Brown 80
Baird's Suruga Bay
Imperial IPA 64
Baxbier Koud Vuur 143
Beavertown Gamma Ray 67

Belgium

Boon Oude Geuze
Mariage Parfait 126
Brasserie de la Senne
Bruxellensis 126
Brasserie Lefebvre Blanche
de Bruxelles 47
Cantillon Lou Pepe Kriek 109
Green's Dry-Hopped
Lager 162
Mikkeller Drink'in The Sun 165
Orval 125
Oud Beersel Kriek 103
Rochefort 10: 152
Rodenbach Grand Cru 127
St Bernardus ABT 12: 152
Tilquin Oude Gueuze à
l'Ancienne 125

Bernard Free Sour Cherry 161
Bieres Goutte d'Or
Ernestine 63
Boon Oude Geuze
Mariage Parfait 126
Brasserie de la Senne
Bruxellensis 126
Brasserie du Bocq,
Blanche de Namur 47
Brasserie du Mont
Blanc la Blonde 91
Brasserie Lefebvre
Blanche de Bruxelles 47

Brazil

2 Cabeças/Cevejaria Dadiva
Pink Lemonade 105
Bodebrown Black Rye IPA 139
Ceveja Morada
Hop Arabica 93
Eisenbahn Weizenbier 52
Seasons Basilicow 95
Way Witbier 55

C

Calavera Beer Mexican
Imperial Stout 97
Calvors Dark Dunkel Lager 31
Camden Gentleman's Wit 48

Canada

Brasserie Dieu du Ciel
Peche Mortel 154
Glutenberg American
Pale Ale 163
Unibroue Ephemere 107

China

Baird's Suruga Bay
Imperial IPA 64

Czech Republic

Bernard Free Sour Cherry 161
Pilsner Urquell 27

D

De Molen Weer & Wind 154

Denmark

Hornbeer Top Hop 39
Mikkeller Drink'in The Sun 165
Dugges All The Way 40

E

Edge Brewing Ziggy 38
Eisenbahn Weizenbier 52
Elgood's Coolship Dark 127
Erdinger Alkoholfrei 166

F

Fentiman's Lemon
Shandy 166
Feral Brewing Co. White 48
Firestone Walker Pivo 29
Five Points Pils 23
Forst Felsenkeller 25
Founder's All Day IPA 37
Fourpure Session IPA 37

France

Bieres Goutte d'Or
Ernestine 63
Brasserie du Mont
Blanc la Blonde 91
Brasserie Duyck Jenlain
Ambrée 117
Brasserie Pietra Colomba 53
Brasserie St Germain &
Nøgne Ø Rhub'ipa 108
La Choulette Biere
des Sans Culottes 117
Sainte Cru Tempete
du Desert 69

G

Garage Project Hapi Daze 40

Germany

Aecht Schlenkerla
Rauchbier Märzen 77
Arcobräu Urfass
Alcohol-Free 165
Augustiner-Bräu Dunkel 31
Ayinger Celebration 81
Erdinger Alkoholfrei 166
Himburg's Braukunst
Keller Bavarian Dry
Hop Lager 29
Köstritzer Schwarzbier 28
Original Ritterguts Gose 131
Schneider Weisse Meine
Hopfenweisse Tap 5: 51

H

Hackney Red 79
Harvey's Sussex Best 83
Harviestoun Ola Dubh 155
Himburg's Braukunst
Keller Bavarian Dry
Hop Lager 29
Hitachino Nest White Ale 49
Hornbeer Top Hop 39

I

Ireland

The White Hag Little Fawn
Session IPA 41

Italy

Birra del Borgo Duchessa 119
Birrificio del Ducato Verdi 145
Forst Felsenkeller 25
Le Baladin Wayan 119
Tipo Pils 27
The Wall Brewery Salty
Amber 76

J

Japan

Hitachino Nest White Ale 49
Ise Kadoya Brown Ale 83
Minoh W-IPA 68

K

The Kernel Export
India Porter 139
Köstritzer Schwarzbier 28

L

La Choulette Biere
des Sans Culottes 117
La Cumbre Beer 24
La Sirène Praline 137
Lagunitas Daytime Ale 38
Le Baladin Wayan 119
Leeds Brewery Original
Pale Ale 162
Lervig/Magic Rock
Farmhouse IPA 118
Little Creatures Rogers' 76
Lost Abbey Duck
Duck Gooze 129
Lost And Grounded Running
With Sceptres 25

M

Magic Rock Inhaler 69
Marble Brewery
Damage Plan 62

Mexico

Calavera Beer Mexican
Imperial Stout 97
Cerveceria Agua Mala
Session IPA 41

N

Naparbier Hefeweizen 52
Neptune Brewery Abyss 138

Netherlands

Baxbier Koud Vuur 143
Brouwerij Martinus
Smoked Porter 144
De Molen Weer & Wind 154
Grutte Pier Barrel Aged
Tripel With Brett 129
Jopen Jacobus RPA 85

Ramses Naar de Haenen 94
Texels Bock 81
Two Chefs Brewing
White Mamba 95

New Zealand
8 Wired Feijoa 109
Croucher New Zealand
Pilsner 23
Garage Project Hapi Daze 40
Good George Rocky Road 144
North End Brewing Amber 85
Renaissance Brewing
Tribute 155
Tempest Brewing Co. Long
White Cloud 63
Yeastie Boys Gunnamatta 92
North End Brewing Amber 85

Norway
Amundsen Bryggeri Dessert
In A Can Chocolate
Marshmallow 141
Brasserie St Germain &
Nøgne Ø Rhub'ipa 108
Lervig/Magic Rock
Farmhouse IPA 118

O
Oakham Citra 65
Odell Cutthroat Porter 138
Original Ritterguts Gose 131
Orval 125
Oud Beersel Kriek 103

P
Pilsner Urquell 27
Pirate Life IPA 61

R
Ramses Naar de Haenen 94
Renaissance Brewing
Tribute 155
Robson's Wheat Beer 55
Rochefort 10: 152
Rodenbach Grand Cru 127
Rogue Sriracha Hot Stout 97

S
Sainte Cru Tempete
du Desert 69
Savour Saison 91
Schneider Weisse Meine
Hopfenweisse Tap 5: 51
Seasons Basilicow 95
Sierra Nevada Torpedo 61
Siren Yulu 92
Ska Brewing Pinstripe
Red Ale 84

South Africa
Cape Brewing Company
Krystal Weiss 51
Devil's Peak King's
Blockhouse 62
Robson's Wheat Beer 55
Standeaven Watermelon
Lager 93

Spain
Dougall's 942: 39
Edge Brewing Ziggy 38
Naparbier Hefeweizen 52

Sweden
Dugges All The Way 40
Thornbridge & St Erik's
Imperial Raspberry Stout 107

Switzerland
7 Peaks La Dent Jaune 24

T
Tempest Brewing Co.
Long White Cloud 63
Terrapin Rye Pale Ale 79
Texels Bock 81
Thornbridge & St Erik's
Imperial Raspberry
Stout 107
Thornbridge Lukas 28
Three Floyds Gumballhead 53
Tilquin Oude Gueuze
à l'Ancienne 125
Tipo Pils 27
Two Birds Bantam IPA 68
Two Chefs Brewing
White Mamba 95

U
Unibroue Ephemere 107

United Kingdom
Anspach & Hobday
Smoked Brown 77
Beavertown Gamma Ray 67
Big Drop Chocolate
Milk Stout 161
Brew By Number
Motueka & Lime 115
Burning Sky Saison
à la Provision 116
Calvors Dark Dunkel Lager 31
Camden Gentleman's Wit 48
Durham Brewery
Temptation 143
Elgood's Coolship Dark 127
Fentiman's Lemon
Shandy 166
Five Points Pils 23

Fourpure Session IPA 37
Fuller's Imperial Stout 141
Fuller's Vintage 153
Fyne Ales Vital Spark 145
Hackney Red 79
Harvey's Sussex Best 83
Harviestoun Ola Dubh 155
JW Lees Harvest Ale 153
The Kernel Export
India Porter 139
Leeds Brewery Original
Pale Ale 162
Lost And Grounded
Running With Sceptres 25
Magic Rock Inhaler 69
Marble Brewery
Damage Plan 62
Moor Raw 75
Neptune Brewery Abyss 138
Oakham Citra 65
Savour Saison 91
Siren Yulu 92
Tempest Brewing Co. Long
White Cloud 63
Thornbridge & St Erik's
Imperial Raspberry
Stout 107
Thornbridge Lukas 28
Victory Brewing Uncle
Teddy's British Bitter 75
Westerham Brewery Co.
Scotney Pale Ale 163
Wild Beer Co Wild
Goose Chase 118
Williams Bros. Kelpie 94
World Top Against
The Grain 167

USA
10 Barrel Brewing
Cucumber Crush 131
21st Amendment Hell
or High Watermelon 104
Alesmith Nut Brown Ale 80
Anchor Steam Beer 84
Bagby Beer Three
Beagles Brown 80
Bell's Two Hearted 67
Boulevard Tank 7: 115
Captain Lawrence Brewing
Effortless Grapefruit
IPA 104
Cigar City Marshal Zhukov's
Penultimate Push 137
Crooked Stave Surrette
Provision Saison 116
Firestone Walker Pivo 29
Founder's All Day IPA 37
Funkwerks Raspberry
Provision 103

Goose Island Bourbon
County Stout 151
Green Flash Le Freak 64
La Cumbre Beer 24
Lagunitas Daytime Ale 38
Lost Abbey Duck
Duck Gooze 129
New Belgium Glütiny
Golden Ale 167
New Holland Dragon's
Milk 151
Odell Cutthroat Porter 138
Rogue Sriracha Hot Stout 97
Sierra Nevada Torpedo 61
Ska Brewing Pinstripe
Red Ale 84
Terrapin Rye Pale Ale 79
Three Floyds Gumballhead 53
Wicked Weed Genesis 105
Young Henrys Mulberia 108

V
Victory Brewing Uncle
Teddy's British Bitter 75

W
The Wall Brewery
Salty Amber 76
Way Witbier 55
Westerham Brewery Co.
Scotney Pale Ale 163
The White Hag Little
Fawn Session IPA 41
Wicked Weed Genesis 105
Wild Beer Co Wild
Goose Chase 118
Williams Bros. Kelpie 94
World Top Against
The Grain 167

Y
Yeastie Boys Gunnamatta 92
Young Henrys Mulberia 108

MAIN INDEX

Recipe titles are in *italics*

8 Wired Brewery 109
21st Amendment Brewery 104

A
Acetobacter 17
alcohol-free beers 159, 161, 165, 166
   big float 169
amber ales 73, 76, 85
Anspach & Hobday 77
asparagus with Session IPA hollandaise foam 42
Augustiner-Brau 31

B
bacteria 17
bacterial fermentations 123
Bagby Beer 80
Baladin Brewery 119
barley 12
barley wines and food 19
batter: *beery tempura* 32
Bax Bier 143
beasts 17
Beavertown 67
beef: *proper corned beef* 98
beer and food 18–19
Berliner Weisse 17, 19
Bières de Garde 113, 117
big beers 149
   mega malt loaf 156
Big Drop Brewing Co. 161
Big Drop Chocolate Milk Stout: *big float* 169
bitters 18, 73, 75
Bjergsø, Mikkel Borg 165
black lagers 21, 28
bock 81
Bodebrown Brewery 139
botanicals 89, 90–7
Boulevard Brewing Company 115
bourbon: *saison julep* 121
Brasserie de la Senne 126
Brasserie du Mont Blanc 91
Brasserie Duyck 117
Brasserie Lefebvre 47
Brasserie St Germain 108
bread: *simple beer bread* 86
brettanomyces 17
brewer's salts 13
Brooklyn Brewery 51
brown ales 18, 73, 77, 80, 83
   simple beer bread 86
Burning Sky Brewery 116
Burton-on-Trent: water 13

C
cakes: *mega malt loaf* 156
Calavera Beer 97
Camden Town Brewery 48
Cerveza Dougall's 39
Ceveja Morada 93
cherries: *duck with Flanders cherry sauce, potatoes and greens* 132
chicken: *gluten-free beer brined chicken kiev* 168
cocktails
   beerita sunrise 33
   big float 169
   my Thai 99
   Ninkasi's kiss 133
   peat nut monster 147
   a quick session 43
   rubeicon 111
   saison julep 121
   a sly gin 57
coffee beers 93
colour 12
cooking with beer 18–19
coolships 123, 127
corned beef: *proper corned beef* 98
Croucher Brewery 23
crumpets: *it's always crumpet season* 120
cuckoo breweries 92, 93
custard: *mild custard* 146

D
dark beers 135, 137–45
   mild custard 146
   peat nut monster 147
dark lagers 31
De Molen Brewery 154
duck with Flanders cherry sauce, potatoes and greens 132
Dunkels 21, 31

E
Elgood's Brewery 127
Erdinger Brewery 166

F
farmhouse beers 113, 115–19
   it's always crumpet season 120
   saison julep 121
Firestone Walker 29
Flanders red ales and food 19
Flanders-style beer: *duck with Flanders cherry sauce, potatoes and greens* 132
flavour 12, 18–19
food pairing 18–19

Fourpure Brewery 37
fractional IPAs 38
fruit beers 101, 103–9
   rubeicon 111
   tingly oysters 110
fruit, dried: *mega malt loaf* 156
Fuller's Brewery 141, 153
Fyne Ales Brewery 145

G
Garage Project 40
Germany: Beer Purity Law 16
Geuze-style beers 129
gin: *a sly gin* 57
ginger beer: *big float* 169
glasses 149
gluten-free beers 159, 162, 163, 167
   gluten-free beer-brined chicken kiev 168
Glutenberg Brewery 163
golden ales and food 18
Good George Brewing 144
Goose Island Brewery 151
Goses 57, 131
grains 12
grapefruit juice
   IPA and grapefruit vinaigrette 70
   a quick session 43
Green Flash Brewing Company 64
Green's Brewery 162
Guinness 135

H
Hackney Brewery 79
herb beer 89, 90–7
   proper corned beef 98
Hitachino 49
hollandaise sauce: *asparagus with Session IPA hollandaise foam* 42
hops 14–15, 52, 59, 64, 65
Hymn to Ninkasi 16

I
ice cream
   big float 169
   orange beer ice cream 56
imperial stouts 17, 141
   peat nut monster 147
IPAs 13, 18–19, 37, 68, 139
   IPA and grapefruit vinaigrette 70
Ise Kadoya Brewery 83

J
JW Lees Brewery 153

K
Kelpie: *proper corned beef* 98
Köstritzer Brewery 28
kriek beer: *tingly oysters* 110

L
La Cumbre Brewing Company 24
La Sirène Brewery 137
Lactobacillus 17
lagering 21
lagers 18, 21, 23–31
   beerita sunrise 33
   beery tempura 32
   gluten-free 162
Lagunitas 38
lambic-style beers 17, 123, 127
lambics 123, 126
lemonade: *beerita sunrise* 33
liquor 13
London: water 13
Lost Abbey Brewery 129
Lost and Grounded Brewery 25
Lucca Cafés Especiais de Curitiba 93
lychee liqueur: *rubeicon* 111

M
Magic Rock Brewery 69
malt and malting 12
malt loaf: *mega malt loaf* 156
Marble Brewery 62
Maris Otter 12
Mikkeller Brewery 165
mild beer: *mild custard* 146
milk stouts
   alcohol-free beers 161
   big float 169
Moor Beer Company 75

N
Naparbier 52
New Belgium Brewing Company 167
Nøgne Ø 108
North End Brewing 85

O
Odell Brewing Company 138
Oktoberfests 21, 31
old ales and food 19
orange beer ice cream 56
Orval Brewery 125
Orval: *Ninkasi's kiss* 133

...d Beersel 103
  tingly oysters 110
oysters: *tingly oysters* 110

P

pale ales 18, 163
pale malts 27
peanut butter: *peat nut monster* 147
Pediococcus 17
Pilsen 27
Pilsner 21
Pilsner Urquell Brewery 27
porters 13, 17, 138

R

recipes
  asparagus with Session IPA hollandaise foam 42
  beery tempura 32
  duck with Flanders cherry sauce, potatoes and greens 132
  gluten-free beer-brined chicken kiev 168
  IPA and grapefruit vinaigrette 70
  it's always crumpet season 120
  mega malt loaf 156
  mild custard 146
  orange beer ice cream 56
  proper corned beef 98
  simple beer bread 86
  tingly oysters 110
red ales 19, 73, 79, 84
Renaissance Brewing Company 155
Rheinheitsgebot 16
Ritterguts Brewery 131
Rochefort Brewery 152
Rodenbach Grand Cru: *duck with Flanders cherry sauce, potatoes and greens* 132

S

Saisons 17, 113, 115, 116, 118, 119
  it's always crumpet season 120
  saison julep 121
Schneider Weisse Brewery 51
Schneider Weisse Meine Hopfenweisse: *a sly gin* 57
seafood: *beery tempura* 32
session beers 35, 37–41
  asparagus with Session IPA hollandaise foam 42

a quick session 43
Sierra Nevada Brewery 61
Ska Brewing 84
Sorachi Ace (hops) 52
sours and food 19
spiced beer 89, 90–7
  my Thai 99
Stone & Wood Brewery 65
stouts 19, 151
  alcohol-free beers 161
  peat nut monster 147

T

tea: *mega malt loaf* 156
Tempest Brewing Co. 63
tempura: *beery tempura* 32
tequila blanco: *beerita sunrise* 33
terroir 14–15
Texels Brewery 81
Thornbridge Brewery 28, 107
Three Floyds Brewery 53
Trappist beer 125, 152
Two Birds Brewery 68
Two Chefs Brewing 95

V

vegetables: *beery tempura* 32
vermouth: *Ninkasi's kiss* 133
vinaigrette: *IPA and grapefruit vinaigrette* 70
vodka
  my Thai 99
  a quick session 43

W

The Wall Brewery 76
water 13
Way Brewing Company 55
Wayan: *it's always crumpet season* 120
weizens 45, 49, 51
wheat beers 18, 45, 47, 165
  alcohol-free beers 165, 166
  orange beer ice cream 56
  a sly gin 57
whisky: *peat nut monster* 147
white ales 49
The White Hag Brewery 41
Wicked Weed Brewery 105
Wild Beer Co. 118
wild beers 123, 127
  duck with Flanders cherry sauce, potatoes and greens 132
  Ninkasi's kiss 133
Williams Bros. 94
witbier 45, 48

Y

Yeastie Boys 92
yeasts 16, 123

THE LITTLE BOOK OF

CRAFT BEER

MELISSA COLE

First published in 2017 by Hardie Grant Books, an imprint of
Hardie Grant Publishing

Hardie Grant Books (UK)
52–54 Southwark Street
London SE1 1UN

Hardie Grant Books (Australia)
Ground Floor, Building 1
658 Church Street
Melbourne, VIC 3121

hardiegrantbooks.com

British Library Cataloguing-in-Publication Data. A catalogue
record for this book is available from the British Library.

ISBN: 978-1-78488-115-3

Publisher: Kate Pollard
Commissioning Editor: Kajal Mistry
Editorial Assistant: Hannah Roberts
Cover and Internal Design: Stuart Hardie
Copy editor: Kay Halsey
Proofreader: Kate Berens
Indexer: Cathy Heath
Colour Reproduction by p2d
Printed and bound in China by 1010